CITYSPOTS
PRAGU

Carolyn Zukowski

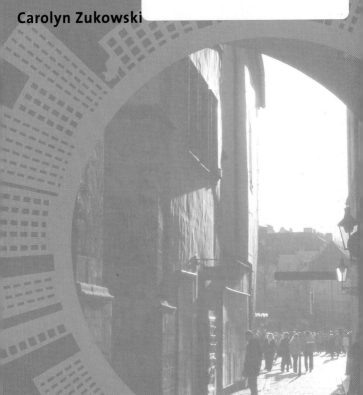

Written by Carolyn Zukowski
Original photography by Carolyn Zukowski, Helena Zukowski, Czech Tourism
Front cover photography © Walter Bibikow/www.photolibrary.com
Series design based on an original concept by Studio 183 Limited

Produced by Cambridge Publishing Management Limited
Project Editor: Rachel Wood
Layout: Julie Crane
Maps: PC Graphics
Transport map: © Communicarta Ltd

Published by Thomas Cook Publishing
A division of Thomas Cook Tour Operations Limited
Company Registration No. 1450464 England
PO Box 227, Unit 18, Coningsby Road
Peterborough PE3 8SB, United Kingdom
email: books@thomascook.com
www.thomascookpublishing.com
+ 44 (0) 1733 416477
ISBN-13: 978-1-84157-641-1
ISBN-10: 1-84157-641-7

First edition © 2006 Thomas Cook Publishing
Text © 2006 Thomas Cook Publishing
Maps © 2006 Thomas Cook Publishing
Series Editor: Kelly Anne Pipes
Project Editor: Ross Hilton
Production/DTP: Steven Collins

Printed and bound in Spain by GraphyCems

CONTENTS

SYMBOLS & ABBREVIATIONS

The following symbols are used throughout this book:

ⓐ address   ☏ telephone   ☏ fax   ⓔ email   ⓦ website address
🕒 opening times   Ⓝ public transport connections   ⓘ important

The following symbols are used on the maps:

🄸 information office		◯	city
✈ airport		◯	large town
✚ hospital		◦	small town
🛡 police station		═	motorway
🚌 bus station		─	main road
🚆 railway station		─	minor road
Ⓜ metro		─	railway
✝ cathedral			
❶ numbers denote featured cafés & restaurants			

Hotels and restaurants are graded by approximate price as follows:
£ budget   **££** mid-range   **£££** expensive

● *A Prague night can't wait to begin*

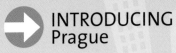

INTRODUCING
Prague

Introduction

Think of Disneyworld, with its colourful attractions, fun houses, quaint miniature squares and breathtaking amusement rides. Now take away the dazzling customer service, cut the price of an entrance ticket in half, add lots of alcohol and cigarettes, and put a bureaucrat in control. It sounds absurd, but that's Prague (*Praha* in Czech). And it's precisely what has attracted artists, alchemists, anarchists and travellers to Prague for centuries.

While Prague's classical music and the Czech Republic's unmatched beer are among some of the best reasons to visit, the primary pleasure for many is simply strolling Prague's moody cobblestone streets and enjoying the unique atmosphere, rain or shine. Exquisite examples of a thousand years of European architecture are crammed together on the twisting narrow streets of this city that many travellers regard as 'the Europe that I wanted to see when I came to Europe'.

To limit uncontrolled development and to ensure that Prague retains its postcard perfect beauty for centuries to come, the City of Prague declared the core of the city the Prague Heritage Reserve. In 1992, UNESCO joined the effort, declaring the city centre a World Heritage Site. With the inclusion of the Czech Republic into the EU in 2004, being a tourist here couldn't be easier or more satisfying.

It's fitting that the word *práh*, in Czech, means threshold. Prague is the gate to the centre of Europe, bridging the gap between old and new. As you sit among the throngs of tables in the Old Town Square, marvelling at the beauty of a thousand spires that has launched a million tour groups, you will witness the absurd minutiae of daily life – the supermodel who serves you at the hot dog stand, the medieval-costumed minstrels talking on their mobile phones, or the artistic splash of graffiti on a Romanesque building. Prague's open-door policy couldn't be more apparent. So keep your eyes open, and enjoy the ride. You will be coming back for more.

🔺 *Prague, a graceful collision of old and new*

When to go

SEASONS & CLIMATE

Prague's geographical location in the northern part of central Europe allows for some mercurial weather patterns. This only adds to the romantic nature of this beautiful city, which is well equipped to keep visitors comfortable all year round. Most public transport is heated and air-conditioned and, whenever the weather turns foul, there's always a good pub or café around the next corner. The average temperature in December and January is 5°C (41°F). In the hottest months, June and July, the temperature usually hovers at around 30°C (86°F).

ANNUAL EVENTS

There is always something happening in Prague. Here is a list of yearly events, but check www.pis.cz or www.prague-info.cz for the most current events schedule in English. Buy tickets in advance online for many of these at Ticketpro. ⓦ www.ticketpro.cz

January–March

Prague Winter Festival First week in January. A week of classical music served up in some of Prague's most sumptuous interiors. ⓦ www.praguewinterfestival.com

One World International Film Festival Beginning of March. One of the leading festivals in Europe dealing with the issue of human rights. ⓦ www.jedensvet.cz

Febiofest End of March. Now the largest audiovisual showcase in Central Europe, the week-long independent film festival features more than 500 movies from 50 countries in 15 cinemas around Prague, many with English subtitles. ⓦ www.febiofest.cz

April–June

Velikonoce (Easter) A strange Czech rite of spring. On Easter Monday, boys carefully weave a willow switch, and give their girlfriends a swat with it, thereby ensuring the girls' health for the coming year. The girls, in exchange, give the boys a painted egg, or a swatch of ribbon to tie onto their willow switch.

Khamoro End of May. International festival of gypsy culture. If you like to dance hard, this is your venue. ⓦ www.khamoro.cz

Prague Spring Music Festival 12 May–3 June. This world-famous series of classical music and dance performances begins with the anniversary of Bedřich Smetana's death on 12 May. Symphony, opera and chamber performances bring some of the world's best talent to Prague. Tickets are available in advance (beginning in December) from Hellichova 18, Praha 1. ⓦ www.festival.cz

World Festival of Puppet Art End of May, beginning of June. Marionettes, puppets and their masters make this one of the most wonderfully creepy events in Prague. ⓦ www.puppetart.com

Dance Prague June. International festival of contemporary dance and movement theatre. ⓦ www.tanecpha.cz

July–September

Shakespeare Summer Festivities June–September. The Burgrave Palace in the Prague Castle complex brings these plays as well as your inner thespian to life. ⓦ www.shakespeare.cz

Prague Autumn International Music Festival September–October. A great chance to see some of the most famous Czech and international orchestras in one of Prague's most beautiful venues, the Rudolfinum. ⓦ www.pragueautumn.cz

Strings of Autumn September–November. This classical music festival draws heavily on the relationship of classical music and

theatre, with famous personalities thrown in for good measure.
ⓦ www.strunypodzimu.cz

October–December
International Jazz Festival Last week in October. A celebration
of jazz music, held in several venues across town.
ⓦ www.jazzfestivalpraha.cz
Anniversary of the Velvet Revolution 17 November. Watch the
president lay a wreath at the small bronze 'free hands' monument
hanging on the wall near Národní trída 20.

🔺 *A wintry view from the Prague castle steps*

Advent and Christmas 5–26 December. St Mikuláš, the Czech version of St Nick, dressed in a white bishop's costume, kicks off the season on 5 December by giving sweets to good children and coal and potatoes to the naughty ones. Just before Christmas, local fishmongers bring in carp by the barrelful while market stalls selling hot mulled wine or grog dot the city, drawing everyone into the Christmas mood.

New Year's Eve 31 December. Give the embattled centre of Prague a miss during the New Year's Eve, or Silvestr, festivities, and go for spectacular views of fireworks and a mellower pace at Prague Castle or Vyšehrad.

PUBLIC HOLIDAYS

DATE	HOLIDAY/ANNUAL EVENT	CZECH NAME
1 Jan	New Year's Day	Nový rok
Apr	Easter Monday	Pondělí velikonoční
1 May	Labour Day	Svátek práce
8 May	Liberation Day	Den osvobození
5 July	SS Cyril and Methodius	Den Cyrila a Metoděje
6 July	Jan Hus Day	Den Jana Husa
28 Sept	Czech Statehood Day	Den válečných veteranů
28 Oct	Independence Day	Den vzniku Československa
17 Nov	Struggle for Freedom & Democracy Day	Den boje za svobodu a demokracii
24 Dec	Christmas Eve	Štědrý den
25 Dec	Christmas Day	Boží hod vánoční
26 Dec	Boxing Day	2. svátek vánoční

Tapping the market

It's the classic David and Goliath tale, with a little globalisation thrown in. Budějovické, or 'Budweis' (in German) beer comes from the Czech city of České Budějovice, where it has been brewed since the 13th century. Nineteen years before the Czech company, Budvar, began bottling in České Budějovice, a German-born American immigrant, Adolphus Busch, started to produce his Budweiser beer in St Louis in 1876. Busch declared the product the King of Beers, and registered the trademark Budweiser in the US.

There was no problem until both companies started looking to sell their product internationally and clashed at a trade fair at the turn of the 20th century. In 1911 they came to an understanding; Budvar agreed not to sell their beer north of the Panama Canal and Budweiser agreed to stay out of Europe. This worked well until the

fall of the Berlin wall, when the possibility of breaking into new international markets became appealing to both sides.

'We have no problem with Budvar selling their beer. They just can't use names too close to ours', say the Budweiser execs in the US. The Czech Budvar team retorts: 'Budějovice (Budweis) has been producing beer since 1260; before the US even existed!' Neither company relishes the prospect of consumers mistaking their product as something produced by the other, though the dispute is probably helping the much smaller Budvar more than hindering it. Budvar admits that the long-running battle has had a beneficial effect, defining its brand strategy and enabling it to tap new markets that otherwise might have been much harder to penetrate by keeping the brand fresh in people's minds and giving them something to talk about in the pub. A case of any publicity is good publicity.

 Roll out the barrel

History

The city has been influenced, and at times overrun, by people from all points of the compass, including Celts, Slavs, Romans, Poles, Jews, Germans and Russians, to name a few. Communists and capitalists as well as hundreds of artists, alchemists and architects have left their mark on 'the city of a hundred spires', 'the new Left Bank' and 'the Bohemian capital'.

In the mid-14th century, Prague was the centre of the Holy Roman Empire and Europe's third largest city in terms of population. The reign of Charles IV was a Golden Age in Czech history. The end of this period, however, brought economic and political strife to the area as Protestant Hussites – inspired by the ideas of the religious reformer Jan Hus – battled it out with crusaders sent by the Catholic church in the 15th century.

The Austrian Habsburgs captured the Bohemian throne in the 16th century, which left Bohemia as part of the Austrian Empire for 400 long and sombre years, until the end of World War I. The Habsburgs were repressive rulers, except for the brief but bright reign of the mentally unstable Emperor Rudolf II. He surrounded himself with gifted astronomers such as Tycho Brahe and Johannes Kepler, while alchemists such as John Dee stirred mysterious vats in the castle kitchens and exotic animals strolled through the corridors.

● *Architectural detail in St Vitus Cathedral*

At the end of the 18th century, the Enlightenment reforms of Maria Theresa and her son, Josef II, led to the Germanisation of the country. It wasn't long before the Czechs began to express their desire for self-determination. The Czech National Revival movement was born, and aspired to reintroduce Czech language and culture; it soon began to strive for political emancipation as well.

On 28 October 1918, an independent Czech and Slovak state formed in Prague after the Austro-Hungarian defeat in World War I. This new country, led by President Tomáš Garrigue Masaryk, experienced a boom and Czechoslovakia became one of the ten richest nations in the world.

The Nazi occupation of Bohemia and Moravia was disastrous for Czechoslovakia, leaving only the country's beautiful buildings unscathed. After World War II, the restored Czechoslovak Republic fell under Soviet influence. An attempt to reform and humanise the Communist system, known as the Prague Spring, failed miserably when Russian forces invaded the country in August 1968. The 1970s and 1980s were stifled times for many Czechoslovaks, who created their own dissident counter-culture.

Mass protests and demonstrations in Prague led to the bloodless overthrow of the Communist regime in November 1989, also known as the Velvet Revolution. Václav Havel, a dissident playwright, became president of the new democratic republic. On 1 January, 1993, because of 'irreconcilable differences', the Czechoslovak state was divided into independent Czech and Slovak republics. Years of financial mismanagement left the city in disrepair, and capitalists soon took on the task of renovating it to its former beauty.

The Czech Republic joined the European Union in 2004, and today's Prague is once again on the rise, rebuilding its repressive past into a vibrant future.

Lifestyle

The Czech population is incredibly diverse, from tram-riding
*babička*s wearing headscarves to Zen youths eating macrobiotic
dishes at one of Prague's new organic restaurants. Twenty years ago,
the city lost many of its skilled hopefuls to emigration but, over the
last few years, an influx of immigrants and returning Czech émigrés
has made Prague more interesting than ever. Many Czechs have a

● *Staré Město after a few beers*

German, Hungarian, Polish, Romany, Slovakian or Vietnamese background. You might think this would breed tolerance, but there still exists a certain xenophobia on the part of some Czechs. There may not be any open hostility in the city, but neither is there an atmosphere of inclusiveness and multiculturalism. Visitors of Asian or African origin may find the stares uncomfortable, although there is almost never any kind of physical threat. This situation should improve as the economic situation improves and more Czechs start travelling.

The Czechs are generally well educated and seem to have a better grasp of mathematics, history and world geography than their similarly educated European counterparts. In Prague you will find many young people who are very eager to practise their English. There is also a general aptitude and affinity for music and art, resulting in some excellent metro graffiti and fantastic impromptu musical performances in pubs.

During the hot months of summer, you may find that there aren't that many Czechs around. Don't take it personally; Czechs often leave their apartments in the city for their *chata* or *chaloupka* in the country on the weekends. These tiny country houses are a great way to take advantage of the beautiful countryside. Many Czechs are great gardeners and nature enthusiasts, knowing which wild mushroom is edible, and exactly which part of a slaughtered pig is the tastiest.

When in Prague, bear in mind that your holiday represents a luxury that the average citizen, earning around 22,000 Kč a month, does not have. Remarking loudly, 'Wow, this (fill in the blank with: beer, knick-knack, bus trip, meal) is SO CHEAP!', is perhaps not the most sensitive approach. What you may consider cheap is, for many Czechs, still a luxury.

Culture

For a city of little more than one million, Prague packs in enough museums, art galleries, theatres and opera houses to provide a lifetime of entertainment.

Prague has a proud history of supporting culture. It's a city of artistic innovation and tolerance, and has provided appreciative audiences to musicians such as Mozart and writers like Franz Kafka. The most important cultural landmark in Prague is the Národní divadlo (National Theatre). Built at the birth of the Czechoslovak nation, when there was a need to create a national identity using Czech language, music and drama, the Národní divadlo represented the cultural life Czechs wanted for themselves. Today the National Theatre oversees three ensembles: the National Opera, the National

Ballet and the National Drama Company, which perform at some of the most beautiful venues in town, namely the National, Estates and Kolowrat Theatres.

Prague Spring (Pražské jaro) is Prague's best-known annual cultural event, where the festival venues are as big a draw as the music. It begins on 12 May, the anniversary of Smetana's death, with a procession from his grave at Vyšehrad to the Obecní dům (Municipal House), followed by a performance of his *Má vlast* song cycle.

For a typically Czech theatrical experience, you can choose from three distinctive performance genres, all of which are great for visitors, as they are language-free and held at central locations. Visually stunning 'black light theatre' stories are told using elements of mime, modern dance, ballet, animated film, and acting or

⬇ *So much to see, so little time*

puppetry bathed in light on a dark background. Marionette theatre is another Czech tradition offering wonderful puppet performances of pieces ranging from Mozart's famous *Don Giovanni* to the Beatles' *Yellow Submarine*. Laterna Magika is a uniquely Czech mix of film, visual effects, sound and ballet. Always evolving, the themes are fresh and exciting, and performances are well worth the entrance ticket.

The Czech film tradition embodies the history of the Czech Republic: rise, repression, rebellion and rebirth. Prague's Film and Television School of the Academy of Performing Arts and the Barrandov Studios have a long and distinguished history. They produced some 80 films a year from the 1930s until the Soviet invasion in August 1968. Privatised after the fall of Communism, Barrandov Studios no longer received funding from the government. The 1990s saw the rise of a new generation of Czech film-makers, including Jan Svěrák and Jan Hřebejk. Svěrák's Oscar-nominated *Elementary School* (*Obecná škola*, 1991) and Oscar-winning *Kolya* (*Kolja*, 1996) as well as Hřebejk's Oscar-nominated *Divided We Fall* (*Musíme si pomáhat*, 2000) are excellent examples of modern Czech films dealing with historical themes.

Now, foreign film-makers have discovered Prague as an attractive location due to its beautiful surroundings, undamaged architecture, relatively low filming costs and expert local crews. To support the growing number of foreign film projects, local production companies as well as companies providing casting, lighting, editing and special effects services have been established. Many Czech films have English subtitles, so it's worth going to see one while you're in Prague.

● *A view from the Vltava towards Prague castle*

MAKING THE MOST OF
Prague

Shopping

Prague's mix of high-end fashion, low-brow kitsch and home-grown market stalls holds appeal for just about everyone, but if you want to buy luxury clothing or electronics, you will probably find them cheaper in the UK. For antiques buffs, Prague has dozens of antiquarian book shops that can yield some excellent finds. Many *bazar*s (second-hand shops) have interesting supplies of old linens, mirrors, brooches and crystal beads.

Nearly every *papírnictví* (stationery shop) has beautiful watercolour and coloured-chalk sets that make perfect gifts. Other top trinkets include small bottles of emerald green absinthe, Bohemian crystal, colourful necklaces, funky and occasionally tacky nesting dolls, garnet jewellery and ceramic goods.

The main shopping areas are pedestrianised Na příkopě, at the foot of Václavské náměstí (Wenceslas Square), lined with mid-range international retailers, and Národní (National) Street. Celetná is the souvenir strip, while the area between the Old Town Square and

● *Na příkopě dressed for winter celebrations*

Karlův most (Charles Bridge) is packed with small, winding streets that contain the city's highest concentration of shops. Check out Charles Bridge, where you'll find quirky, small kiosks.

There are two permanent markets in Prague: Havelské Tržiště, the main open-air market in Old Town, featuring a good selection of fruit and vegetables, artwork, leather goods, flowers, wooden toys and ceramics; and Pražská Tržnice, with outdoor market stalls that sell just about everything. Both attract a large crowd of locals and tourists. Haggling is best left until the end of the day, when the sellers are more receptive to offers.

Havelské Tržiště (Havel's Market) ⓐ Havelská ul ⓒ 06.00–18.30 Mon–Fri, 08.00–18.00 Sat & Sun ⓝ Metro: Můstek

Pražská Tržnice (Prague Market) ⓐ Holešovice ⓒ 08.00–18.00 Mon–Fri, 08.00–13.00 Sat, closed Sun ⓝ Metro: Vltavská, then Tram: Pražská Tržnice

USEFUL SHOPPING PHRASES

What time do the shops open/close?
Kdy obchody otevírají/zavírají?
Gdee obkhodee ohteveerahyee/zavveerayee?

How much is this?
Kolik je to?
Kollick yeh toh?

Can I try this on?
Můžu si to vyzkoušet?
Moozhoo see toh veezkowshett?

My size is ...
Moje velikost je ...
Moye vellickost yeh ...

I'll take this one, thank you.
Koupím toto, děkuji pěkně.
Kowpeem totoh, dekujee pyeknye.

Eating & drinking

Pivo (beer) is the lifeblood of this metropolis, and you'll be hard-pressed to find anyone who doesn't imbibe the occasional half-litre. The beer-drinking tradition started in the Middle Ages, a direct response to water pollution; brewing and filtering the beer seemed to kill off most of the bugs. Today, Czech beer has an alcohol level of between 4 and 5 per cent, and people stick to their favourite brands, swearing lifelong allegiance to the pub that serves it. A beer has to look just right when it comes to you, with a thick, frothy head, and it must be cool, not cold. A proper Pilsner takes seven minutes to pour. The best brands are Bernard, Gambrinus, Kozel, Pilsner Urquell, Staropramen and Radegast. To really feel at home in Prague, you need learn just one simple phrase: *Ještě jedno pivo prosím* ('One more beer, please').

Czech cuisine does not offer much choice for vegetarians, but most people will probably find at least a couple of meals to their liking, including *bramboračka* (potato soup), *vepřové knedlíky a zelí* (traditional roast pork with dumplings and sauerkraut), *ovocné knedlíky* (fruit-filled dumplings with cream or special sweet cheese) or *jablečný závin* (apple strudel). Czech cooking and eating habits have been shifting towards a healthier lifestyle, but traditional Czech recipes with their rich sauces and condiments are still extremely popular. If this isn't your cup of tea, then don't despair; Prague has some good organic, vegetarian and ethnic restaurants. Check the listings in the *Prague Post* for the latest reviews.

If you choose to eat in a pub rather than a tourist restaurant, you'll probably spend no more than £10 for your soup, main course and drink. Try *svíčková*, a dish of tender beef covered in an orange

❶ *Beer is the national drink*

cream sauce topped with cranberries, cream and a slice of lemon.
Bread dumplings often accompany the meal and the trick is not to
leave one speck of sauce. For vegetarians, *smažený sýr* (fried cheese)
is hot with chips and tartare sauce and sometimes even a bit of
greenery. If you want a really cheap meal on the go, try a *párek v
rohlíku* (hot dog with ketchup and/or mustard) or a *langoš* (fried
dough with garlic, cheese or cinnamon sugar on top). You can find
fast-food kiosks on just about any street corner in Prague.

As for drinks, if you're not in the mood for beer, you can have
minerálka (mineral water), *pomerančový džus* (orange juice) or
jablečný džus (apple juice). Czechs also like to drink *čaj* (tea) and *kava*
(coffee) with or without *mléko* (milk) or *smetana* (cream). For an
after-dinner treat, sip a Moravian brandy of the *slivovice* (plum) or
meruňkovice (apricot) varieties.

Most restaurants in Prague have a menu in English. The
expected tip for good service is between 5 and 10 per cent, but if you
get the typically Czech 'service with a scowl', you can forget the tip.

There are numerous supermarkets in Prague if you prefer
picnicking to eating out. Tesco on Národní Třída is a good bet, since
it's all familiar, but go to any *potraviny* (local grocery), and try your
hand at getting some of the nicest *šunka* (ham), *salám* (salami) or
sýr (cheese). *Rohlíky* (small white bread baguettes) or *chleba* (rye or
whole wheat bread) are very tasty with *máslo* (butter).

PRICE RATING

The restaurant price guides given in this book indicate the
approximate cost of a three-course dinner without drinks.
£ Budget 300 Kč; ££ Mid-range 500 Kč; £££ Expensive 700 Kč

USEFUL DINING PHRASES

I would like a table for ... people.
Přeji si stůl pro ... osob.
Przheyee see stool proh ... ossobb.

May I have the bill, please?
Přeji si platit, prosím?
Przeyee see platteet, prosseem?

Could I have it well-cooked/medium/rare, please?
Přeji si to dobře propečené/středně/jen lehce propečené,
prosím?
*Przeyee see toh dobrzeh proppecheneh/strzednyeh/yen lehtseh
proppecheneh, prosseem?*

I am a vegetarian. Does this contain meat?
Jsem vegetarián. Není v tom maso?
Ysem vegetahreeahn. Nenyee ftom mahsoh?

Where is the toilet (restroom) please?
Kde je záchod, prosím vás?
Gdeh yeh zakhod, prosseem vahs?

I would like a cup of/two cups of/another coffee/tea.
Přeji si šálek/dva šálky/ještě jednu kávu/ještě jeden čaj.
*Przeyee see shahleck/dvah shalckee/yeshtye yednoo kahvoo/
yeshtye yedenn chay.*

Entertainment & nightlife

As soon as you hit town, buy the English language weekly, *Prague Post*, at any newspaper stand, sit down at a café and make your plan of attack. The 'Night & Day' section is thick with cultural offerings; on any day of the week, you can attend high-brow classical performances, see sticky-floored grunge shows or club the night away.

CINEMA

Prague has over 30 *kino* (cinemas), some showing first-run international films, some showing Czech films. Admission costs anywhere from 90 Kč to 160 Kč. Full listings are published in the 'Night & Day' section of the *Prague Post*. Hollywood blockbusters may be dubbed into Czech, but films are usually shown in their original language; *anglický verze* means 'English version' and *české titulky* means 'Czech subtitles'.

CLUBS & BARS

Most of Prague's dance clubs cater to the young MTV Europe crowd who want to hear techno/tribal beats. Most venues open late (after 21.00) and keep the music going until 04.00 or 05.00. But some of the most popular and interesting scenes in Prague are the alternative and experimental venues that combine theatres and clubs with an underground look and feel. There you'll find bands, DJs, drama, dance, art and films under one roof. Some of the best are the Roxy (see page 78) and the Palác Akropolis (see page 122).

Clubs are to be found all over Prague, but each area has its own certain style. For a more up-market tipple, try the Malá Strana area, where jazz and cocktails mix with the lamplight and smoky alleyways. For a more eclectic mix of performance art while nuzzling your neighbour and guzzling beer, try Josefov and the Old Town. The glittery club scene is most attractive in the New Town. For a night

● *The ever-popular Radost Café*

you won't remember, the Žižkov and Vinohrady areas have a great mix of places, ranging from grungy local hang-outs to sleekly designed gay and lesbian bars that stay open late and don't charge steep cover.

MUSIC

Along with the dedicated concert halls, Prague's many churches and Baroque palaces also serve as performance venues, staging choral performances, organ recitals, string quartets, brass ensembles and occasionally full orchestras. You can get details of these concerts from PIS (Prague Information Service) offices (see page 151). If you go to a concert in a church, remember to take an extra layer of clothing, even on a hot summer day.

TICKETS

For most events, even the ones that are 'sold out', you can often get tickets at the box office half an hour or so before show time. Most performances have a certain number of tickets set aside for VIP guests and visitors, so take a chance and you may be rewarded with the show of a lifetime. Most venues offer discounts for students, children and the disabled.

If you want to be sure of a seat, try a ticket agency. Their advantage is convenience; they accept credit cards and you can book from abroad using their website. Ticketpro is the biggest agency, with branches in PIS (Prague Information Service) offices and many other places around town.

Ticketpro Main Office ⓐ Rytířská 12, Prague 1 ⓣ 296 333 333 ⓦ www.ticketpro.cz ⓛ 09.00–20.00

◀ *Art nouveau splendour at the Obecní dům*

Sport & relaxation

SPECTATOR SPORTS

Despite its small size, the Czech Republic has produced some big names in the sporting world, including Dominik Hašek, Jaromir Jagr, Ivan Lendl, Martina Navrátilová and Pavel Nedvěd.

The most popular competitive sports in the country are football and ice hockey. AC Sparta Praha (Sparta Prague) is one of the most popular and successful football clubs in Europe. The ice hockey team, HC Slavia Praha (Slavia Prague), is world class. The teams play at the T-Mobile or Paegas Arena, and at the Sazka Arena. Wherever you go, you will have as much fun watching the spectators as the game itself. You can buy advance tickets for games through www.ticketpro.cz

The Hockey Club Sparta ⓐ T-Mobile Arena, Za elektrarnou 419
ⓦ www.hcsparta.cz
Hockey and Football Club Slavia ⓐ Sazka Arena, Ocelářská 2
ⓦ www.hc-slavia.cz

PARTICIPATION SPORTS

Prague is a city that you can actively enjoy at any time of the year. Scenic strolls along the river are popular, and there are plenty of restful oases in the parks and squares but there are many other ways to enjoy the city. Whether it's from the back of a bike or the table of a masseuse, Prague is the perfect backdrop for whatever activity you choose.

Biking

In the warmer months, try a guided tour with **City Bike**. It's best to go at the end of the day when the traffic has thinned out and the smog has cleared. ⓐ Kralodvorska 5 ❶ 776 180 284 ❷ tours leave at 10.00, 14.00 & sunset ⓝ Metro: Nám. Republiky

Praha Bike runs similar two-and-a-half-hour tours of the city. ⓐ Dlouhá 24 ❶ 732 388 880 ⓝ Metro: Staroměstská

Boating

Renting a rowing boat or pedalo on the Vltava river will give you an interesting new perspective on the city. You'll find boat rentals open every day from April to the end of October, from 09.00 to nightfall under Charles Bridge, directly across from Club Lávka, or on Slovanský Ostrov. ⓝ Metro: Staroměstská or Malostranská

Fitness and spa treatments

Treating yourself to a massage or a spa treatment is very reasonable – and you know you're worth it!

Cybex Health Club and Spa ⓐ Prague Hilton, Pobřežní 1 ❶ 224 842 375 ⓦ www.cybexprg.cz ❷ 07.00–22.00 ⓝ Metro: Florenc

World Class Fitness Centre ⓐ Václavské nám. 22 ❶ 234 699 100 ⓦ www.worldclassfitness.net ❷ 08.00–21.00 ⓝ Metro: Muzeum

Walking tours

On a walking tour of the city you will discover secret spots that you may never have seen without a guide.

The Insider Tour ⓦ (www.praguer.com ⓝ Metro: Muzeum) covers all the city highlights and offers complimentary refreshments and a ride on the funicular. Tours leave daily from the statue at the top of Václavské náměstí (Wenceslas Square) at 9.45 and 13.30.

Prague Walks (ⓦ www.praguewalks.com ⓝ Metro: Staroměstská) has a good range of walks, all leaving from the Old Town Hall.

Accommodation

The bad news is that accommodation in the centre of Prague is no longer the cheap sleep that travellers bragged about ten years ago. The good news is that Prague's swift and reliable public transportation makes almost any out-of-the-way place an easy hop, skip and jump to the centre.

If you still wish to stay in the centre, the most conveniently located rooms are in the Old Town, Lesser Quarter and Castle District, and command the best views with the biggest price tags. Old Town addresses can be less than peaceful due to revellers staggering home after a night out, so check the actual location of your accommodation, or have a look at the room, if possible, before making a commitment. The districts of New Town, Holešovice and Vyšehrad all offer less pricey accommodation and are also convenient for all the sights. If you are staying for more than a few days, it can be a good idea to book a conveniently located apartment with all the amenities through an accommodation agency (see below).

Cheaper options are plentiful, whether you wish to stay in a *penzion*, hostel or camping ground. The word *penzion* means 'bed and breakfast accommodation', although the breakfast may consist of only coffee and rolls with butter. Some of the new hostel-type accommodation will surprise you with their modern facilities, good locations and friendly service. For nature-lovers, or those on a particularly tight budget, there are many camping sites around Prague, where you can expect to spend 100–200 Kč a night for the right to pitch your tent, and about 350 Kč a night to park your caravan.

PRICE RATING

The ratings below indicate the approximate cost of a double room including breakfast per person per night.

£ Budget 500 Kč; ££ Mid-range 2,000 Kč; £££ Most expensive 4,000 Kč

The rating system in Prague is arbitrary, sometimes dictated by the accommodation owners rather than a controlling body, and the price that you pay does not always reflect the level of service or the quality of surroundings. For this reason, some visitors like to book their accommodation on arrival rather than pre-booking. It is worth remembering that if you arrive late in the day, you can try asking for a discount on hotel or *penzion* rooms; these establishments would often rather let a room at a discount than have a room go empty. If you want help finding what you're looking for, there are good accommodation-finding agencies in town. Two of the best are:

AVE ⊕ Hlavní nádráží (Main Train Station), Wilsonová 8 ☎ 251 111 091, 24-hour late arrivals helpline 602 180 312

Prague Information Service (PIS) ⊕ Staroměstské náměstí (Old Town Square) & Hlavní nádráží ☎ 12 444 ⓦ www.pis.cz

If you prefer to have your accommodation booked before you leave, AVE's website, www.praguehotellocator.com, offers big internet discounts on some of the nicest hotels in town as well as on budget places to stay. For hostel and backpacker accommodation bookings, www.hostelworld.com is an excellent site.

The following are just some of the most popular places to stay:

HOTELS

Botel Admiral ££ A boat hotel with some great views on the river and easy access to all the sights. ⓐ Hořejší nábř. 57, Smíchov ⓣ 257 321 302 ⓦ www.admiral-botel.cz ⓝ Metro: Anděl

Anděl's Hotel ££ New, modern and sleekly designed, right next to the Novy Smichov shopping centre. ⓐ Stroupežnického 21, Smíchov ⓣ 296 889 688 ⓦ www.andelshotel.com ⓝ Metro: Anděl

Hotel Antik ££ Small, quiet and perfectly located 3-star hotel with lots of nice antique touches and a garden out the back. ⓐ Dlouhá 22, Old Town ⓣ 222 322 288 ⓦ www.hotelantik.cz ⓝ Metro: Nám. Republiky or Staroměstská

Mamaison Residences ££ Luxury, fully equipped apartments in central locations throughout Prague. Central reservation office ⓣ 234 376 376/7 ⓦ www.mamaison.com

Pension Unitas & Art Prison Hostel ££ Friendly and homely non-smoking hotel with wholesome, large breakfasts. The cheaper attached hostel is where political prisoners used to be kept; Vaclav Havel stayed in Room 6. ⓐ Bartolomějská 9, Old Town ⓣ 224 221 802 ⓦ www.unitas.cz ⓝ Metro: Můstek or Narodní Třída

Castle Steps Hotel £££ Friendly, centrally located and boutique as can be, located on the stairs to the castle and within walking distance of all the charming places in Malá Strana. ⓐ Nerudova 10 ⓣ 257 531 941 ⓦ www.castlesteps.com ⓝ Metro: Malostranská

🔺 *The elegant and upmarket Hotel Paříž*

Hotel Paříž £££ Classic art nouveau hotel close to all the main sights; worth the financial splurge. ⓐ U Obecního domu 1, Old Town ⓣ 222 195 195 ⓦ www.hotel-pariz.cz Ⓜ Metro: Náměstí Republiky

Radisson SAS Hotel £££ Central, nicely appointed, with barrier-free access, and all the expected 5-star perks. ⓐ Štěpánská 40, New Town ⓣ 222 820 000, from the US 800 333 3333 ⓔ sales.prague@radissonsas.com Ⓜ Metro: Můstek

HOSTELS
Hostel Elf £ Clean, comfortable rooms with communal kitchens. Just two stops to the centre of Prague in a scruffy (read: interesting) working-class neighbourhood. ⓐ Husitska 11, Žižkov ⓣ 222 540 963

🅦 www.hostelelf.com 🅝 Metro: Florenc, then Bus: 133 or 207 one stop to U Památníku

Miss Sophie's £ Very comfortable, boutique backpackers with friendly staff, specially designed ensuites and a great location. 🅐 Melounova 3 🅣 296 303 530 🅦 www.miss-sophies.com 🅝 Metro: IP Pavlova

Sir Toby's Hostel £ Smoke-free, child- and backpacker-friendly, with spotless rooms oozing character, and a nice common area in the basement. 🅐 Dělnická 24, Holesovice 🅣 283 870 635 🅦 www.sirtobys.com 🅝 Metro: Vltavska, then Tram: Dělnická

CAMPSITES

Intercamp Kotva Only 20 minutes from the centre of Prague, with pitches for tents and hook-ups for caravans and all the facilities you need. 🅐 U ledáren 1557/55, Braník 🅣 244 466 085 🅝 Tram: 3, 16, 17 or 21 to Braník, then walk four minutes towards the river, following the signs

Sunny Camp About 30 minutes from the centre of Prague with lots of green space for tents and caravans. The camp is signposted and just 500 m (¼ mile) from the metro stop. 🅐 Smíchovská 1989, Stodulky 🅣 251 625 774 🅝 Metro: Lužiny

Both of these camping sites can offer spartan accommodation in their on-site *penzion*s if the weather makes tenting seem unappealing.

🅞 *The only thing missing is the red carpet – welcome to Prague*

THE BEST OF PRAGUE

A river meanders through it, and you will want to do the same. Even getting lost on a cobbled sidestreet is part of the city's charm. The most important sights in Prague are centred around the Old Town. Just walking these streets, even if you flounder in the tourist current, will astound you. There are few cities as picture-perfect as Prague.

TOP 10 ATTRACTIONS

- **Josefov (Jewish Quarter)** A spot for quiet reflection among some beautiful historic buildings (see pages 80–93).

- **Karlův most (Charles Bridge)** A vibrant place day or night, bustling with vendors, entertainers, locals and tourists (see page 94).

- **Malá Strana (Lesser Quarter)** Ancient and atmospheric (see pages 94–111).

- **Národní muzeum (National Museum)** A bastion of Czech history and prehistory all under one roof (see page 69).

- **Obecní dům (Municipal House)** An art nouveau dream (see page 60).

- **Petřín Hill and Funicular** A 318 m (1,043 ft) hill covered in eight parks and topped with a 62 m (203 ft) copy of the Eiffel Tower. It offers fabulous views of Prague and the surrounding area (see page 98).

- **Pražský hrad (Prague Castle)** Possibly the largest ancient castle complex in the world, boasting a magnificently elevated cliff-top position, and crammed with artistic and architectural treasures (see page 98).

- **Staroměstské náměstí (Old Town Square)** Studded with cafés and inimitable Baroque, Gothic, and Romanesque architecture, including the Old Town Hall and its exquisite 14th-century Astronomical Clock, St Nicolas Church, and the Jan Hus Monument (see page 62).

- **Týn Church** The final resting place of Tycho Brahe. The lopsided Gothic spires, symbolising the male and female element, are a Prague landmark (see page 64).

- **Václavské náměstí (Wenceslas Square)** The brash Czech Champs-Élysées and the largest and busiest shopping plaza in Prague (see page 66).

◆ *Prague's many bridges*

Your brief guide to seeing and experiencing the best of Prague, depending on the time you have available.

HALF-DAY: PRAGUE IN A HURRY

If you have only a few hours to spare, then concentrate on Hradčany (the Castle District) and Malá Strana (the Lesser Quarter). Visit the Gothic St Vitus Cathedral and St George's Basilica, and pass the Lilliputian houses of Zlatá ulička (Golden Lane). Then descend into Malá Strana where you'll find ancient burgher houses and the Baroque copper-domed St Nicolas Church. Making your way across Charles Bridge can take as little or as much time as you like; if you enjoy souvenir stands, performers, artists, musicians, or just beautiful city views, you may like to linger a while. Once across the bridge, walk along the riverside and join the ranks of famous Czech writers and dissidents who also needed a coffee break at the famous Café Slavia, on Smetanovo nábřeží, where you can sip coffee and enjoy the view over the river and up to the castle on the other side.

1 DAY: TIME TO SEE A LITTLE MORE

After a morning in the Hradčany and Malá Strana areas, make your way from Charles Bridge on the time- and tourist-worn cobblestones to the oldest part of Prague, aptly named Old Town. At its centre is the fabulous Staroměstské náměstí (Old Town Square), home to some of Prague's most famous and beautiful monuments, such as the colourful Orloj (Astrological Clock) and Týn Church. From there, work your way up Celetná ulice towards the Prašná brána (Powder Tower) and the Obecní dům (Municipal House), and from there, walk west along Na příkopě to the tourist mecca that is Václavské náměstí (Wenceslas Square).

2–3 DAYS: SHORT CITY-BREAK

With a bit more time, you'll be able to do everything listed above in more depth, plus spend half a day in Josefov, the Jewish Quarter, with its own pensive and reverent atmosphere. Then visit a gallery or a museum, and maybe take in an evening concert. To keep your energy levels up, sample some wonderfully heavy Czech cuisine from one of the recommended local restaurants.

LONGER: ENJOYING PRAGUE TO THE FULL

Lucky you! Prague is more than just a sightseer's dream; it is a place to be savoured. With more than a few days here, you can get in all of the above sights at a leisurely pace, chill out at some funky cafés or clubs, and take a day trip to Karlštejn or Terezín (see pages 126, 134).

● *St Vitus Cathedral – the perfect place for slaying a dragon*

Something for nothing

Prague is *the* destination for budget travellers, as the whole city is an open-air museum accessible 365 days a year, with free admissi⊙

If you enjoy people-watching, the Jan Hus Monument, in the middle of the Old Town Square, provides the perfect perch to watc⊙

🔵 *Everyone and their dog loves the view from Petřin Hill*

the throngs of tourists. You may even catch some enlightening tour commentary in English from one of the passing groups. An even more lively vantage point is Charles Bridge. Here you can hear amusing conversational snippets, cunning pick-up and convincing hard-sell lines, all set to the sound of street musicians and performers. For a bit of loose change, you can stay and watch for as long as you like.

Some beautiful, central spots in Prague are made for rest and relaxation. The gardens leading up to Petřín Hill, the largest of Prague's parks, are magical on a hot summer's day and are frequented by Frisbee throwers, lovers, and only a smattering of tourists. The view from here is enchantingly spire-filled and the clamour of the city is far away.

Prague's hidden churches and cloisters are often used for musical concerts and, therefore, rehearsals. Slip in through the side door, pay your respects, and, if possible, stay for the angelic acoustics.

For museum-goers, the National Museum offers visitors free admission on the first Monday of the month. When you pick up the *Prague Post*, check for any gallery exhibition openings. If you dress smartly enough, no one will notice you cruising the wine and buffet table.

There is free wi-fi access in many cafés and pubs in the centre of town, though they do expect you to buy at least something to eat and drink while you're surfing the net.

If you want to feel like a local, feed the swans under Charles Bridge. Or, for a tram's-eye view of Prague, take a window seat on the number 22 as it wends its way around the historical gems of the city. For 20 Kč you can ride the tram for up to 75 minutes, plenty of time for a circuit of the whole city.

When it rains

Prague's melancholic beauty seems to increase with inclement weather. Rain, sleet or snow shouldn't dampen your spirits, as so many cultural offerings are located indoors, and the reliable public transport system won't keep you waiting for a ride. And, of course, it never rains in pubs and cafés. If you're happy to brave the weather, fortify yourself with a hot *grog* (mix of rum and hot water with lemon and sugar), grab an umbrella and you'll find that many of the tourist attractions are wonderfully quiet.

A coffee house is always a good choice on a rainy day. Coffee has a firm place in Prague's history; it has been the fuel of Czech literati and dissidents for hundreds of years. The typical Czech coffee house has local newspapers hanging on hooks, a burnished wood interior, lots of cigarette smoke, a crowd of jittery customers, and only one recipe for coffee: *turek*. This Turkish coffee is served in small cups with a thick layer of coffee grounds on the bottom. Then there's the American-inspired bookshop-cum-coffee house, offering frothy lattes, internet access and English literary magazines. Write in your journal, order a steady stream of refreshment, and you can stay as long as you like.

A rainy day is the perfect time to see Josefov, the Jewish Quarter, which lends itself to quiet contemplation, or the National Museum, with its wonderfully moody corridors filled with prehistoric and anthropological exhibits. Also good on a rainy day is the Prague Castle complex, particularly St Vitus Cathedral and the Zlatá ulička, the row of houses where Kafka (patron saint of gloomy weather) lived for a brief stint.

Alternatively, try one of the shopping malls, Palác Flora or Nový Smíchov, which offer a variety of diversions under one roof. Palác

Flora (Metro: Flora) offers IMAX theatre and 120 fashion shops, and Nový Smíchov (Metro: Anděl) provides not only fashionable shops but a multiplex cinema, food court, athletic gym, and the largest game arcade in Prague.

⬥ *Escape the elements in the impressive National Museum*

On arrival

TIME DIFFERENCES

The Czech Republic follows Central European Time, which is two hours ahead of GMT in the summer, and one hour ahead of GMT from the end of October to the end of March. In the Czech summer, at 12.00, the time elsewhere is as follows:

America Eastern Daylight Time 06.00, Central Daylight Time 05.00, Mountain Daylight Time 04.00, Pacific Daylight Time 03.00
Australia Eastern Standard Time 20.00, Central Standard Time 19.30, Western Standard Time 18.00
Britain Summer Time 11.00
New Zealand Standard Time 22.00
South Africa Standard Time 12.00

ARRIVING

By air

Prague's Ružyně airport is 20 km (12 miles) from the city centre. Special airport taxis whisk you to the town centre for about 500 Kč. Pay at the airport taxi information desk in the arrivals hall, and they will issue you a receipt to give to the driver. Alternatively, use the ČEDAZ minibus service (☏ 220 114 296 Ⓦ www.aas.cz ⏱ 05.30–21.30) that runs every half hour between the airport and Náměstí Republiky. Tickets cost 90 Kč (including one piece of luggage, children under 10 free) and are sold by the driver or from the booth in the arrivals terminal. The cheapest way to get into town is on bus number 119, which goes from the airport to Dejvická metro station in about 20 minutes. From Dejvická it is just five stops to the

Muzeum metro station in the centre of town. Buy a 20 Kč transport ticket (plus a 10 Kč one for big bags) at the transport information desk in the arrivals hall or from the coin-operated machine at the airport bus stop, not from the driver. You need to validate the ticket (once for the whole trip) in the yellow stamping machines once you're on board the bus. The 24-hour left luggage facility at the airport costs 60 Kč per item per day.

Prague Ružyně Airport ☎ 220 111 111 🌐 www.prg.aero/en/

By rail

Prague has two main railway stations. Praha Hlavní nádraží (Prague Main Train Station) has a tourist office (🕐 09.00–19.00 Mon–Fri, 09.00–16.00 Sat & Sun) in the centre of the lower hall. There's an ATM on the far left of the lower hall. *Úschovna* (luggage storage) is in the form of either coin-operated lockers (10 Kč for 24 hours) or the guarded luggage depository opposite (60 Kč a day, closed for 30 minutes after 05.30, 12.00 and 17.30). Getting into the centre of town involves one stop on the metro to the Muzeum stop, or a walk up busy Wilsonova.

Trains on the main Berlin–Prague–Vienna/Bratislava route use the second station, Praha Holešovice. The small hall holds the ticket office (🕐 09.00–17.00 Mon–Fri, closed Sat & Sun), luggage storage lockers, an internet café and several exchange and accommodation offices (🕐 06.00–23.00). The Prague Public Transit Co. has an office here (☎ 296 191 817 🕐 07.00–18.00) and the helpful staff can give you all the information you need to navigate your way around. From Holešovice it is just three stops on the metro to the Muzeum station.

For multilingual, quick and friendly service, avoid the queues at the Main Train Station counters and buy your ticket at the Czech

Railways Agency. ⓐ V Celnici 6 ⓣ 972 233 930 ⓦ www.cd.cz
ⓒ 09.00–17.00

For up-to-date train and bus schedules in and out of the country, see www.vlak-bus.cz

🔺 The tower on Petřín Hill is a useful landmark

FINDING YOUR FEET

Prague is a simple city to get around, especially in the centre, which is relatively small and compact. The best way to get the lie of the land is to take the overground trams or just walk. The cobblestones and unevenness of the roads call for comfortable footwear; definitely leave the stilettos at home.

ORIENTATION

The Vltava River runs north–south, dividing the city into east and west. The Charles Bridge is the heart of the city, uniting the delights of Staroměstské náměstí (Old Town Square), Václavské náměstí (Wenceslas Square), Josefov, (Jewish Quarter) and Nové Město

---

IF YOU GET LOST, TRY ...

Excuse me, do you speak English?
Promiňte, mluvíte anglicky?
Prommeenyteh, mlooveeteh anglitskee?

Excuse me, is this the right way to ... the cathedral/the tourist office/the castle/the old town?
Promiňte, jedu/jdu správně do ... katedrála/turistická kancelář/hrad/staré město?
Prommeenyteh, yeddoo/ydoo sprahvnye doh ... katteddrahlah/ tooristitskah kantselahrz/hradd/starreh myestoh?

Can you point to it on my map?
Můžete mi to ukázat na mapě?
Moozheteh mee toh ookahzatt nah mappye?

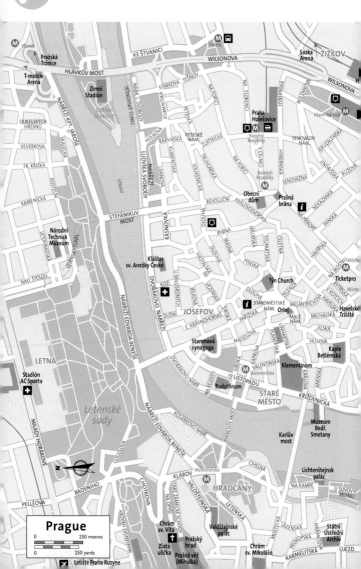

Ruské sady
ITALSKÁ
KRKONOŠSKÁ
ČELAKOVSKÉHO
ŠAFAŘÍKOVA
ANNY LETENSKÉ
Náměstí Míru
URUGUAYSKÁ
AMERICKÁ
JANA MASARYKA
NÁDRAŽÍ
ŠPANĚLSKÁ
NA SMETANCE
MÁNESOVA
ITALSKÁ
VINOHRADSKÁ
BELGICKÁ
ZÁHŘEBSKÁ
VINOHRADY
Český rozhlas
BALBÍNOVA
ANGLICKÁ
LONDÝNSKÁ
BRUSELSKÁ
Státní Opera
VINOHRADSKÁ
JUGOSLÁVSKÁ
BELEHRADSKÁ
BĚLEHRADSKÁ
LUBLAŇSKÁ
KOUBKOVA
LUBLAŇSKÁ
WENZIGOVA
WASHINGTONOVA
Národní muzeum
VOCELOVA
LEGEROVA
OPLETALOVA
Muzeum
MEZIBRÁNSKÁ
P. Pavlova
SOKOLSKÁ
NUSELSKÝ MOST
VÁCLAVSKÉ NÁM.
KRAKOVSKÁ
ŽITNÁ
HÁLKOVA
NA BOJIŠTI
KE KARLOVU
HORSKÁ
Můstek
VÁCLAVSKÉ NÁMĚSTÍ
VE SMEČKÁCH
JEČNÁ
KE KARLOVU
VYŠEHRAD
ŠTĚPÁNSKÁ
V TŮNÍCH
NA RYBNÍČKU
KATEŘINSKÁ
VODIČKOVA
V JÁMĚ
VINIČNÁ
STUDNIČKOVA
PALACKÉHO
ŠKOLSKÁ
NAVRÁTILOVA
ŘEZNICKÁ
ŽITNÁ
LIPOVÁ
Botanická zahrada
APOLINÁŘSKÁ
ALBERTOV
HORSKÁ
JUNGMANNOVA
NA SLUPI
VLADISLAVOVA
Novoměstská radnice
LAZARSKÁ
JEČNÁ
U NEMOCNICE
BENÁTSKÁ
NA SLUPI
VNISLAVOVA
NESLOVOVA
Národní třída
SPÁLENÁ
Karlovo Náměstí
KARLOVO NÁM.
SVOBODOVA
OSTROVNÍ
VÁCLAVSKÁ
VYŠEHRADSKÁ
NÁ MORÁŇ
VRATISLAVOVA
ČERNÁ
MYSLÍKOVA
ŘEMENCOVA
ODBORŮ
VOJTĚŠSKÁ
V JIRCHÁŘÍCH
PŠTROSSOVA
NA ZDERAZE
Klášter Na Slovanech (Emauzy)
TROJICKÁ
POD SLOVANY
VYŠEHRADSKÁ
NÁRODNÍ
GORAZDOVA
DIVIŠ
PODSKALSKÁ
PLAVECKÁ
NA HŘBITŮ
Národní divadlo
MASARYKOVO NÁBŘEŽÍ
Mánes
Žofín
Slovanský Ostrov
Karlovo Náměstí
RAŠÍNOVO NÁBŘEŽÍ
MOST LEGIÍ
JIRÁSKŮV MOST
Vltava
PALACKÉHO MOST
HOŘEJŠÍ NÁBŘEŽÍ
Střelecký Ostrov
Dětský Ostrov
SVORNOSTI
SMÍCHOV
Petřín Hill & Funicular to Prague Castle
VÍTĚZNÁ
JANÁČKOVO NÁBŘEŽÍ
ZBOROVSKÁ
LÍDICKÁ
STAROPRAMENNÁ
JINDŘICHA PLACHTY
VLTAVSKÁ
Justiční palác
ZBOROVSKÁ
MALÁTOVA
KOŘENSKÉHO
V BOTANICE
MATOUŠOVA
NA BĚLIDLE
LÍDICKÁ
OSTROVSKÉHO
PLASKÁ
ŘÍČNÍ
ÚJEZD
EL. PEŠKOVÉ
PRESLOVA
NÁDRAŽNÍ
Anděl
ŠTEFÁNIKOVA
Petřínské sady
MALÁ STRANA

(New Town) to the beauty of Malá Strana (Lesser Quarter), Petřín Hill and Hradčany (Castle District).

Note that building numbers are on blue plaques above the main door, but are not always in consecutive order.

GETTING AROUND

Most of the sights listed in this book are easily accessible on foot, but Prague's efficient, fast and clean public transport system is a good choice if you need to speed across town. With three metro lines, more than twenty tram routes and nine night trams, you won't need to bother with inner-city buses. If you plan to use a lot of transport or can't be bothered fiddling about with change and tickets, you can pay 80 Kč for a one-day pass, 220 Kč for a three-day pass or 280 Kč for a weekly pass. Children under 6 travel free, and children under 15 pay half-price. You will need to buy a 10 Kč ticket for a large backpack or luggage. Remember to validate your ticket by stamping it once at the outset of your journey in the yellow machines at metro entrances and on trams. Failure to do so will earn you a 500 Kč on-the-spot fine from one of the many transport controllers. A controller must show you a gold badge with the metro authority symbol on it as identification. Some tourists have been conned by fake controllers.

Muzeum metro station is the junction for the green and red metro lines and is the centre of the Prague metro system. **Florenc** metro station (pronounced *florence*) is the junction for the yellow and green lines and is where the main bus station is located. **Hlavní Nádraží** metro station is where you will find the Main Train Station.

◗ *Prague's thoroughly modern metro*

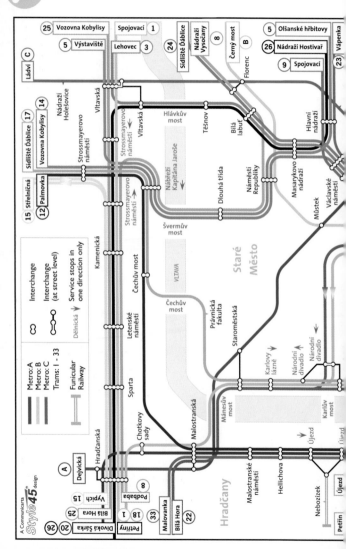

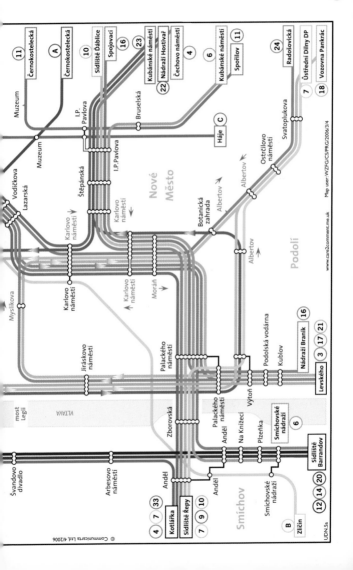

There has been a crackdown on unscrupulous taxi drivers recently, and there is now much better control of meters. However, it is always safest to ask your waiter or hotel receptionist to call you a taxi. From the airport to town, expect to pay anywhere between 500 and 700 Kč. It costs 30 Kč to step into a taxi, and then a rate of 22 Kč for a kilometre or for every two minutes thereafter. AAA Radiotaxi (❶ 140 14 or 222 333 222) is consistently one of the best companies.

CAR HIRE

If you are staying in Prague, it makes no sense to rent a car. If, however, you decide to do a couple of day trips, this is a good option. Most foreign driving licences are valid, including those issued in Canada, the USA and the EU. In the city, the speed limit is 50 km/h, outside urban areas it's 90 km/h, and 130 km/h on highways. Seatbelts are compulsory in the front and back seats. You can find rental car agencies directly outside the airport on the ground floor of the airport parking garage and in the city centre.

The following rental companies are generally open on weekdays from 07.00–21.00. Many close or have reduced hours at weekends. It makes sense to check out their websites as you can often get better deals online.

A-Rent Car ❶ 224 211 587 Ⓦ www.arentcar.cz
Alimex ❶ 220 114 860 Ⓦ www.alimexcr.cz
Avis ❶ 221 851 225 Ⓦ www.avis.cz
Czechocar CS ❶ 220 113 454 Ⓦ www.czechocar.cz (offering one-way rental to many Czech cities)
Europcar ❶ 224 811 290 Ⓦ www.europcar.cz
Sixt ❶ 220 115 346 Ⓦ www.e-sixt.cz

❷ *The Powder Tower and the Municipal House, an unlikely coupling*

THE CITY OF
Prague

Staré Město (Old Town) & Nové Město (New Town)

The Old and New Towns of Prague are just that; a combination of old and, well, not quite so old. In Old Town, more than a thousand years of history is captured by its modern visitors as they photograph the beauty of its old-world alleyways, Baroque balconies and candy-coloured façades. New Town isn't new at all. It was founded in 1348 by Charles IV, and is the bustling commercial centre of Prague, blending tradition with innovation, low-end trinket shops with high-end boutiques tucked into art nouveau buildings, all clamouring for your business. Make sure your money belt is secure and your bags zipped, as this is the rip-off route where pickpockets target tourists.

SIGHTS & ATTRACTIONS

Start your tour of the Old and New Towns from the **Prašná brána (Powder Tower)**. This was built in 1475 by King Vladislav Jagiello on the site of a 13th-century fortified tower and is an official gateway to Old Town. Later, the tower was used to store gunpowder, hence its name. You can tour its innards daily from 1 March to 1 October, hours vary. Ⓜ Metro: Náměstí Republiky

The Royal Court, where the kings of Bohemia used to stay from the late 14th century onwards, was once located where the art nouveau **Obecní dům (Municipal House)** stands today. Built between 1905 and 1910, it has been beautifully restored to its former glory and now holds a Czech and French restaurant, a excellently-appointed café, a gallery, shop and classical music venue. This Fabergé egg of architecture was the site for two major Czech events;

Staré Město & Nové Město

| 0 | 250 metres |
| 0 | 250 yards |

Kláster sv. Anežky České & Národní Galerie v Praze

RÁSNOVKA

LANNOVA

KLIMENTSKÁ

BARVÍŘSKÁ

DUŠNÍ

U MILOSRDNÝCH

JOSEFOV

BÍLKOVA

Dům U černé Matky boží

DLOUHÁ

SOUKENICKÁ

PETRSKÉ NÁM.

Staronová synagoga

HAŠTALSKÁ

REVOLUČNÍ

ZLATNICKÁ

TRUHLÁŘSKÁ

NA POŘÍČÍ

Rudolfinum

NA REJDIŠTI

ŠIROKÁ

VEZENSKÁ

Národní Galerie v Praze

MASNÁ

RYBNÁ

JAKUBSKÁ

Náměstí Republiky

V CELNICI

NESOUV MOST

17 LISTOPADU

ŠIROKÁ

MASELNA

PAŘÍŽSKÁ

Staroměstská

KAPROVA

Jan Hus Monument

DLOUHÁ

STUPARTSKÁ

Obecní dům

Masarykovo Nádraží

STARÉ MĚSTO

VALENTINSKÁ

PLANÉRSKÁ

Týn Church

CELETNÁ

Prašná brána

HYBERNSKÁ

SENOVÁZNÁ

SENOVÁŽNÉ NÁM.

lův st

Klementinum

KARLOVA

LINHARTSKÁ

Staroměstské NÁM.

Staroměstská radnice

MALÉ NÁM.

Orloj

Dům U kamenného zvonu

Carolinum

NA PŘÍKOPĚ

NEKÁZANKA

JINDŘIŠSKÁ

Hlavní Nádraží

Muzeum Bedř. Smetany

ANENSKÁ

HUSOVA

MICHALSKÁ

MELANTRICHOVA

Sex Machines Museum

Ovocný trh

Muzeum Komunismu

Muchovo Muzeum

Náprstkovo muzeum Asijských, Afrických a Amerických kultur

KONVIKTSKÁ

Kaple Betlémská

BETLÉMSKÁ

HAVELSKÁ

V KOTCÍCH

RYTÍŘSKÁ

Stavovské divadlo

PANSKÁ

PŘÍKOPĚ

RŮŽOVÁ

VLADISLAVOVA

Mûstek

Mûstek

JUNGMANNOVA

NÁRODNÍ

PALACKÉHO

Václavské NÁM.

Muzeum

Národní divadlo

OSTROVNÍ

OSTROVNÍ

VORŠILSKÁ

V JIRCHÁŘÍCH

Národní třída

VODIČKOVA

OPLETALOVA

WASHINGTONOVA

Státní Opera

Žofín

MASARYKOVO NÁBŘEŽÍ

CÉRNÁ

LAZARSKÁ

ŠTĚPÁNSKÁ

VE SMEČKÁCH

KRAKOVSKÁ

MEZIBRANSKÁ

Národní muzeum

Mánes

NAVRÁTILOVA

Novoměstská Radnice

ŘEZNICKÁ

ŠKOLSKÁ

V JÁMĚ

KREMENCOVA

MYSLÍKOVA

ODBORŮ

ŽITNÁ

ŽITNÁ

NA RYBNÍČKU

VÍTŮNŮ

HALKOVA

SOKOLSKÁ

RESSLOVA

Karlovo Náměstí

JEČNÁ

JEČNÁ

P. Pavlova

VOCELOVA

BĚLEHRADSKÁ

Tančící dům

NA ZDERAZE

VÁCLAVSKÁ

VYŠEHRADSKÁ

TROJANOVA

RUMUNSKÁ

Metro Stop
Cathedral
Information
Police Station
Airport
Railway Stn
Bus Station
Hospital

NA MORÁNI

NOVÉ MĚSTO

U NEMOCNICE

KATEŘINSKÁ

KE KARLOVU

NA BOJIŠTI

Botanická zahrada

BENÁTSKÁ

VINIČNÁ

APOLINÁŘSKÁ

the declaration of the Czechoslovakian State was staged in 1918, and, in 1989, the Civic Forum discussed the Velvet transfer of power and the state's transformation into a democratic republic. ❸ nám. Republiky 5 ⓦ www.obecni-dum.cz ⓝ Metro: Náměstí Republiky

As you follow along the historic street, **Celetná**, you are tracing the ancient city walls. Over the centuries, the ground level has sunk by several metres, so examples of the earliest existing architecture in Prague, in all its Romanesque charm, are to be found in the cellars of just about every house along the route. Most houses on this street are either wine bars or restaurants, so you are welcome to duck in for a look. House signs, used to identify Prague houses in the past, are still visible on some buildings on Celetná. They are the houses U bílého páva (At the White Peacock ❸ Celetná 10/557), U černého slunce (At the Black Sun ❸ Celetná 8/556) and U bílého lva (At the White Lion ❸ Celetná 6/555). Along Celetná you'll also find the **Ovocný trh (Fruit Market)**. Nearby is where Prague's oldest theatre, namely **Stavovské divadlo (Estates Theatre)**, staged the world premiere of Mozart's opera, *Don Giovanni*, in 1787. Not far from here stands the **Carolinum**, once a college of Charles University founded by Charles IV, comprising several buildings in the Gothic style. **Dům U černé Matky boží** (House at the Black Mother of God ❸ Celetná 34/569) is one of the best-known examples of Cubist architecture in Prague, designed by the architect Josef Gočár and built in 1911–12. It houses a permanent exhibition of Czech Cubism.

The approach from Celetná to **Staroměstské náměstí (Old Town Square)** is, in a word, breathtaking. The huge 1.7-hectare (4-acre) square hosts a constant hum of activity, day and night, and is usually full of tourists gazing at the pleasing blend of carefully restored Gothic, Renaissance, baroque and neoclassical buildings. A popular activity is to rent a horse and buggy with driver and cruise around town in style, or you can just watch the impromptu musical performances and browse the market stalls. The Old Town Square has a long history as centre stage for so many of the city's defining moments, from the execution of Protestant leaders in 1621 to the attacks on Soviet tanks with Molotov cocktails in 1968. The centrepiece of the square is the **Jan Hus Monument**, a memorial to the founding father of the Hussite movement. Towering above the

🔺 *Prague's stunning Old Town Square*

square, half-hidden behind a row of houses, is the fairy-tale turreted
Týn Church. You will notice that the turrets are different;
characteristically Gothic, they symbolise male and female elements.
Inside the church are Late-Gothic and Baroque altars and the grave
of Tycho Brahe, a Danish astronomer who found refuge in the courts
of Rudolf II and spent a lot of time debunking the backward
planetary beliefs of the Middle Ages by making precise astronomical
measurements of the solar system and more than 700 stars.

Staroměstská radnice (Old Town Hall), is fronted by the **Orloj**, an
astronomical clock that serves as the meeting place in Prague for
tourists and locals. As the hour strikes, Jesus and his disciples lead a
pageant that includes the allegorical figures of Death, the Turk, the
Miser, the Fool and the Proud Rooster. It is certainly worth a look if
you can be there on time, but don't miss the climb or lift up the
Town Hall tower itself; for the small admission charge, you will
be rewarded with some stunning views. ❸ Staroměstské náměstí
🕐 09.00–18.00 Tues–Sun, 11.00–18.00 Mon Ⓜ Metro: Staroměstská

Covering an area of over 2 hectares (5 acres), the **Klementinum**
sits in the historic centre of Staré Město. The wondrous maze of
beautifully decorated buildings was completed in the early
1700s by the Catholic church as a college complex devoted to the
re-education of the mostly Protestant Bohemians. The most
impressive buildings are the magnificent Baroque National Library,
complete with vast numbers of manuscripts and old books as well
as a gorgeous decorative interior, the lavishly adorned Chapel of
Mirrors, where Mozart once played and chamber music concerts are
now performed, and the Astronomical Tower, topped with a statue
of Atlas. In 2007, the 'eighth wonder of the medieval world', the

❿ *The fairy-tale turrets of Týn Church*

Codex Gigas, also known as the Devil's Bible, is to be exhibited in the library. The work of one Bohemian monk, who, to atone for his sins, made this massive 75-kg (165-lb) document in one night with the help of one of Satan's minions, will be loaned back to Prague by the Stockholm Royal Library. The manuscript was originally stolen from Prague by Swedish troops during the Thirty Years War (1618–48). ⓐ Mariánské náměstí 4 ⓣ 221 666 311 ⓦ www.nkp.cz ⓛ library 09.00–19.00 Mon–Sat ⓜ Metro: Staroměstská

Tančici dům (Dancing House) was built in co-operation with the American architect Frank Gehry on a vacant riverfront plot next to a building owned by Václav Havel, the Czech playwright and former president, whose strong support for avant-garde architecture was instrumental in getting the controversial design approved and built (though he moved out of his building once construction began). Locals call the house 'Fred and Ginger', since it vaguely resembles a pair of dancers. The house stands out among the neo-Baroque, neo-Gothic and art nouveau buildings for which Prague is famous. Although the building isn't open to the public, there is the highly rated French restaurant, La Perle de Prague (ⓣ 221 984 160), on the roof with magnificent views. ⓐ cnr of Rasinovo nábřeži & Resslova Street ⓜ Metro: Karlovo náměstí

Once a horse market in medieval times, the rectangular-shaped **Václavské náměstí (Wenceslas Square)** is Prague's own Champs-Elysées, dominated at the top of the boulevard by the neo-Renaissance National Museum and surrounded by bars, hotels, shops, cafés, tea houses, restaurants and fast-food stands. At the bottom of the square is the metro stop, Můstek, where a drawbridge once stood, leading to Old Town. Laid out during the reign of Charles IV, the square lies at the very heart of Prague's New Town, serving as a natural focal point for rallies, protests and parades at key moments in the Czech Republic's history. In 1969, the 'Prague Spring' saw a young university student, Jan Palach, set himself alight in protest at the Warsaw Pact invasion, while in 1989, during the Velvet Revolution, huge crowds celebrated the fall of Czech Communism as Václav Havel and Alexander Dubček made a historic proclamation from the balcony of the Melantrich building. From an architectural standpoint there's plenty to see, the art nouveau Hotel Evropa, Wiehl House and Peterkův dům all being prime examples of different period styles. At night, dodgy characters, stag-night party-goers and prostitutes take over, leaving you with the choice to join in or escape to a more quiet part of the city. ⓝ Metro: Můstek or Muzeum

CULTURE

All of the following charge admission:

Dům U kamenného zvonu (Stone Bell House)

The oldest Gothic house in Prague, the Stone Bell House's architectural significance lay hidden to restorers until the 1960s, when they discovered its Gothic origins within the neo-baroque-style building that had been built around it. Today it houses exciting modern art exhibitions run by the City Gallery of Prague.
ⓐ Staroměstská 13 ⓣ 222 327 677 ⓦ www.citygalleryprague.cz
ⓛ 10.00–18.00 Tues–Sun ⓝ Metro: Staroměstská

Rudolfinum

Specialising in modern visual arts, Rudolfinum is an excellent venue for viewing work from internationally renowned artists as well as emerging local talent. These exhibitions are widely publicised, well-attended events, and regularly include seminars, evening tours with commentary and special-interest activities for schools. Have a look at their simple, up-to-date website that provides background on current and future exhibitions. ⓐ Alšovo nábřeží 12 ① 224 893 309 ⓦ www.galerierudolfinum.cz ④ 10.00–18.00 Tues–Sun, closed Mon Ⓜ Metro: Staroměstská

Muchovo muzeum (Mucha Museum)

This museum is dedicated to perhaps the most well-known and admired Czech art nouveau artist, Alfons Mucha (1860–1939). Examples of Mucha's work are visible all over Prague, particularly at the Obecní Dům (Municipal House) and in the gorgeous stained-glass windows at St Vitus Cathedral. The exhibits here include Mucha's paintings, drawings and lithographs as well as his personal belongings. ⓐ Kaunický palác, Panská 7 ① 221 451 333 ⓦ www.mucha.cz ④ 10.00–18.00 Ⓜ Metro: Můstek

Muzeum Komunismu (Museum of Communism)

Ironically wedged between a McDonald's restaurant and a casino, and arranged into three permanent displays – Dreams, Reality and Nightmare – this museum attempts to shed light on the workings of Czechoslovakia's post-war Communist regime, while showing what everyday life was like for Prague's citizens from 1945 to 1989. The exhibits of propaganda, censorship and interrogation are striking. The displays of a hotchpotch of items from school textbooks to border machine guns paint an interesting picture of the era, leaving you with an eerie feeling of familiarity in the light of today's war on terror. ⓐ Na příkopě 10 ① 224 212 966 ⓦ www.muzeumkomunismu.cz ④ 09.00–22.00 Ⓜ Metro: Náměstí Republiky or Můstek

Náprstkovo muzeum Asijských, Afrických a Amerických kultur (Náprstek Museum of Asian, African and Native American Culture)

The Náprstek Museum is a branch of the National Museum and contains exhibitions on North African prehistory, ethnography and ancient Egypt, as well as Native American and Inuit culture. The museum is named after its founder, Vojta Náprstek, who sought to put items brought back by two Czech explorers on public display. ⓐ Betlémská 1 ⓣ 224 497 500 ⓦ www.aconet.cz ⓛ 09.00–12.00 & 12.45–17.30 Tues–Sun, closed Mon Ⓝ Metro: Národní třída or Můstek

Národní Galerie v Praze (National Gallery)

The National Gallery finds its home in many buildings around Prague, and is famous worldwide for its collections. Opening hours for all galleries are 10.00–18.00 Tues–Sun, and Veletržní palác stays open until 21.00 on Thursdays. For a complete listing of exhibitions and events go to www.ngprague.cz

Národní muzeum (National Museum)

The National Museum looms at the top of Wenceslas Square, and is worth a visit if only for its sumptuous interior, complete with magnificent double staircases. There is an exhaustive collection of animals, coins, metals, minerals, bones and fossils, many from Bohemia. ⓐ Václavské nám. 68 ⓣ 224 497 111 ⓦ www.nm.cz ⓛ 10.00–18.00 (summer); 09.00–17.00 (winter); closed first Tues of every month Ⓝ Metro: Muzeum

Sex Machines Museum

Three floors of bizarre and wonderful sex toys used throughout the centuries. Voyeuristic chamber pots, chastity belts, and electric anti-masturbation machines and hand-cranked vibrators give new meaning to bringing the past to life. 🅐 Melantrichova 18 🅣 224 216 513 🅦 www.sexmachinesmuseum.com 🅛 10.00–23.00 🅜 Metro: Můstek

RETAIL THERAPY

Anagram Bookshop Known for its great new and used English language selections. 🅐 Týn 🅣 224 895 737 🅦 www.anagram.cz 🅛 09.30–19.00 Mon–Sat, 10.00–18.00 Sun 🅜 Metro: Staroměstská

C&A You may wish to pay a visit to the company's Prague store now that it is no longer a fixture on Oxford Street in the UK. It is a slightly cramped affair, where locals and tourists alike take advantage of the good value fashions on offer. 🅐 Václavské náměstí 33 🅣 222 811 333 🅦 cs-cz-cw.retail-sc.com 🅛 09.30–20.00 Mon–Sat, 10.00–19.00 Sun 🅜 Metro: Můstek

Černá Růže Shopping Centrum A modern shopping centre on Na příkopě containing a mix of shops, cafés and restaurants. Outlets include Adidas, Bang & Olufsen, Daniel Hechter, Dolce & Gabbana and Mambo. 🅐 Na příkopě 12 🅣 221 014 111 🅦 www.cernaruze.cz 🅛 09.00–20.00 Mon–Fri, 09.00–19.00 Sat, 11.00–19.00 Sun 🅜 Metro: Můstek

Dr Stuart's Botanicus With prime locations in Prague, this chain of natural scent, soap and herb shops is an amazing Anglo-Czech success story. Started by a British botanist and Czech partner on a farm northeast of Prague, Dr Stuart's create sumptuously scented products that make great gifts to take back home. 🅐 Týnský dvůr (behind Týn Church) / Michalská 4, next to Havelské Tržiště ☎ 224 895 446 / 224 212 977 🌐 www.botanicus.cz 🕐 10.00–18.00 Ⓜ Metro: Staroměstská or Můstek

🔺 *Graffitti of the ancients on Staroměstské náměstí*

Dům Hudebních Nástroju This music shop stocks everything from drum kits and bagpipes to pianos and penny whistles. Many of the instruments are made in the Czech Republic, making this a great place for both musicians and memento hunters to explore. ⓐ Jungmannová 17 ☎ 224 222 501 ⏰ 09.00–18.00 Mon–Sat Ⓜ Metro: Můstek or Národní třida

Havelské Tržiště Havel's Market is Prague's best open-air market with fine examples of art, ceramics, leather goods, woodwork, and even a good selection of food items. Give yourself time to browse the stalls. ⓐ Havelská ul ⏰ 06.00–18.00 Mon–Fri, 08.00–18.00 Sat & Sun Ⓜ Metro: Můstek

Jazz Meets World This music shop has a great selection of European jazz artists that are hard to find in mainstream shops. A must-visit for jazz- and ethno-philes. ⓐ Dittrichova 11 ☎ 224 922 830 ⏰ 14.00–18.00 Mon & Fri, 12.00–18.00 Tues–Thur Ⓜ Metro: Karlovo Náměstí

Manufaktura Features unique handicrafts, wooden toys and handmade skincare products. Their home-spun linens are one-of-a-kind. ⓐ Many locations around town, but the main one is at Melantrichova 17 ☎ 221 632 480 Ⓦ www.manufaktura.biz Ⓜ Metro: Můstek

Myslbek Centre This mall is probably the most lavish and well-equipped in Prague, with a good range of shops like Marks & Spencer, Marlboro Classics, Kookai, Calvin Klein, Gant USA and Next, to name a few. There's even a sushi bar. ⓐ Na příkopě 19/21 ☎ 224 239 550 Ⓦ www.myslbek.com ⏰ 09.00–20.00 Mon–Fri, 09.00–21.00 Sat, 11.00–21.00 Sun Ⓜ Metro: Můstek

Promod A favourite with the uptown crowd, this unique French clothing store for women has some excellent bargains on the second floor. ⓐ Václavské náměstí 2 ⓣ 296 327 701 ⓝ Metro: Můstek

RPM: Tamizdat Record Shop Revolutionise your music selection in this incredible shop that focuses on Central and Eastern European indies. The shop is situated in the Unijazz organisation café (head up courtyard stairway number 2 to the fourth floor), where you can have a cup of coffee or beer while listening to their eclectic mix. ⓐ Jindřišská 5 ⓣ 222 240 934 ⓦ www.tamizdat.org ⓛ 14.00–22.00 Mon–Thur, 14.00–21.00 Fri ⓝ Metro: Můstek

Slovanský dům With a prestigious address on Na příkopě, this large complex offers a range of swish shops and boutiques as well as places to eat, drink and relax (read: Thai massage parlour). For movie-goers there's also a state-of-the-art Star City multiplex within the centre. ⓐ Na příkopě 22 ⓣ 221 451 400 ⓦ www.slovanskydum.cz ⓝ Metro: Můstek

TAKING A BREAK

Even in the heat of the tourist season, there are enclaves of quiet within the heart of Old Town, where you can grab a good coffee, a light snack, and relax. Some of Prague's newest eateries cater to the veggie crowd and are refreshingly inexpensive and wholesome – a good foil for the damage done to livers in the evening hours.

Bakeshop Praha £ ❶ This bakery is the absolute best in Prague for cakes, croissants, quiches, and quick customer service. This is mainly a take-away affair, with a few strategically placed stools overlooking

the street. Try the focaccia bread sandwiches and chocolate brownies. ❸ Kozi 1 ☎ 222 316 823 Ⓜ Metro: Náměstí Republiky, then Tram: 5, 8, 14 to Dlouhá třída

Beas Vegetarian Dhaba £ ❷ This Indian vegetarian eatery is popular with locals and tourists alike. Maybe it's the sunny atmosphere, the huge portions and the reasonable prices that keep them coming back for more. ❸ Týnská 19 Ⓦ www.beas-dhaba.cz ⏰ 09.30–20.00 Mon–Sat, 10.00–18.00 Sun Ⓜ Metro: Staroměstská

Café Ebel £ ❸ Directly behind Týn Church is a haven for coffee-shop connoisseurs. If you're in the mood for a strong coffee or frothy latte, this is your best bet. ❸ Týn 2 ☎ 224 895 788 Ⓦ www.ebelcoffee.cz Ⓜ Metro: Staroměstská

Country Life £ ❹ Prague's foremost veggie haven, Country Life is often crowded at lunchtime, but if you go earlier or later, you're sure to find a seat at the cafeteria-style counter. Even non-vegetarians are impressed with the great salads, pizzas and hearty soups, and there's a shop inside where you can stock up for picnics. ❸ Melantrichova 15 ☎ 224 213 366 ⏰ 09.00–20.30 Mon–Thur, 09.00–18.00 Fri, closed Sat & Sun Ⓜ Metro: Můstek

Albio ££ ❺ This is one of the many vegetarian options in the city, although it does serve fish. Albio is a vegan-friendly, organic eatery with an extensive menu featuring good whole foods and organic products from certified Czech organic farms. Wash it all down with

◀ *Frank Gehry's 'Dancing House' stands out among Prague's historic buildings*

Czech-made Bernard beer, an excellent unpasteurised brew.
🅐 Truhlářská 20 Ⓜ Metro: Náměstí Republiky, then Tram: 5, 8, 14, 51 or 54 to Dlouhá třída

Novoměstský Pivovar (New Town Brewery) ££ ❻ This is one of Prague's microbreweries, producing its own light and dark beers. If you are an early riser, you can sample a brew over a hearty breakfast (served from 08.00 onwards); if not, have a beer or two over lunch at the pleasant brewery restaurant. It offers a full range of traditional beer-hall food, and the chance to order a whole suckling pig for large groups. 🅐 Vodičkova ul. 20 ☏ 222 232 448 🅦 www.npivovar.cz 🕐 08.00–23.00 Mon–Fri, 11.30–23.30 Sat, 12.00–22.00 Sun Ⓜ Metro: Můstek

AFTER DARK

Restaurants
Dahab ££ ❼ A combination of tea room, patisserie, café and restaurant, the Dahab offers a range of Middle-Eastern dishes, including vegetarian options, plus hookahs (water pipes) to puff on. Belly dancers really get things going on Thursday, Friday and Saturday nights from 21.30. 🅐 Dlouhá 33 ☏ 224 827 375 🅦 www.dahab.cz 🕐 12.00–01.00 Ⓜ Metro: Náměsti Republiky or Staroměstská

Diwan ££ ❽ A traditional Lebanese eatery. Good hot and cold meze and kebabs, plus an extensive range of meat- oriented main dishes make this restaurant well worth seeking out.
🅐 Na Příkopě 10 ☏ 224 231 515 🅦 www.diwan.cz 🕐 11.30–24.00 Ⓜ Metro: Můstek

Kolkovna ££ ❾ A great Czech restaurant in the centre of town with Pilsner on tap and a beer garden out the back. ⓐ V Kolkovně 8 ⓣ 224 819 701 ⓦ www.kolkovna.cz ⓛ 10.00–24.00 ⓝ Metro: Staroměstská

Restaurace Jáma ££ ❿ Inside this fast-paced American and Tex Mex eatery, you'll find the waitstaff serving up friendly service and the best burgers in town. ⓐ V jámě 7 ⓣ 224 222 383 ⓛ 11.00–01.00 ⓝ Metro: Můstek

Restaurace U mědvídku ££ ⓫ Serves great Bohemian grub, with Budvar on tap and a busy, beer-hall vibe. ⓐ Na Perštýne 7 ⓣ 224 211 916 ⓛ 10.00–23.00 ⓝ Metro: Národní třída

Tulip Café ££ ⓬ One of Prague's newest late-night eating venues with heated garden, café and sports lounge, catering to both locals and expats. Along with a full bar, it serves Pilsner, Gambrinus and Bernard Beer. It serves sophisticated Mediterranean cuisine and American favourites for vegetarians and meat-eaters alike. ⓐ Opatovicka 3 ⓣ 224 930 019 ⓦ www.tulipcafe.cz ⓛ 11.00–24.00 Mon–Wed, 11.00–01.00 Thur–Sat, 11.00–23.00 Sun ⓝ Metro: Národní třída

Bars, clubs & theatres
AghaRTA Jazz Centrum Dark and dingy jazz room featuring top local players every night of the week. ⓐ Železná 16 ⓣ 222 211 275 ⓦ www.arta.cz ⓝ Metro: Muzeum

Duplex A venue offering a combination of nightclub, café and restaurant, Duplex tends to stick to resident DJs. The outdoor

terrace offers a view overlooking the lights of Wenceslas Square.
 Václavské náměstí 21 224 232 319 www.duplexduplex.cz
 Metro: Můstek

Divadlo Archa One of the best-equipped, mid-sized alternative
theatre venues in Europe, featuring interactive shows that utilise
technology, dance and puppetry. If you buy your tickets early,
you can chill out before the show at the Kavarna café next door.
 Na Poříčí 26 221 716 333 www.archatheatre.cz box office
10.00–18.00, theatre 10.00–22.00 Metro: Florenc or Náměstí
Republiky

Laterna Magika (Magic Lantern) Visually stunning multi-media
techniques combine with film and contemporary dance to convey
intriguing and imaginative ideas. Housed in Nová Scéna (part of the
National Theatre, see following listing). Národní třída 4 224 914
129 www.laterna.cz Metro: Národní třída

Národni divadlo (National Theatre) This lavish neo-Renaissance
building on the bank of the Vltava, with its golden crown of chariot-
driving women, is a Czech cultural institution with a rich artistic
tradition. Three artistic ensembles – opera, ballet and drama –
alternate performances in the historic building of the National
Theatre, in the Stavovské divadlo (Estates Theatre) and in the
Kolowrat Theatre. Národní 2 224 901 668
 www.nationaltheatre.cz Metro: Národní třída

Roxy An authentically underground gutted Art Deco building that
continues to be one of the best clubs in town. Funk and techno DJs
spin this place into a frothed-up frolic pad. Arrive around midnight,

when the fun begins. ⓐ Dlouhá 33 ⓣ 224 826 296 ⓦ www.roxy.cz
ⓛ 19.00–24.00 Mon–Thur, 19.00–06.00 Fri–Sun
ⓝ Metro: Náměstí Republiky

🔺 *New Year fireworks in the Old Town*

THE CITY

Josefov

The site of the oldest Jewish settlement in Europe is Prague's haunting historic Jewish Quarter, Josefov, nestled in winding side streets off Maiselova ul., north of the Old Town Square. It is a place where Prague's dark past collides with its fashionable future – where you can almost hear the buildings sinking deeper into their foundations, while decadent culinary and fashion pursuits beckon the visitor to the hidden streets and back alleys.

Named after Emperor Josef II, whose reforms helped to ease living conditions for the Jews, Josefov was once a walled-in area and now holds the historic remains of what used to be a populous ghetto. Only six synagogues, the Ceremonial Hall, the Town Hall and the Old Jewish Cemetery were left standing when the old Jewish buildings were torn down due to neglect, disease and infestation.

CULTURE

Židovské muzeum v Praze (Jewish Museum of Prague)

Founded in 1906 in order to preserve artefacts from the demolition of the many Josefov buildings, the Jewish Museum now houses one of the most extensive collections of Jewish art, textiles and silver in the world. The Nazis closed the museum soon after their occupation of Prague, using the building to hold all the objects they had confiscated from the synagogues in Bohemia and Moravia. During World War II, Jewish artefacts from all over Europe were brought to Prague and stored in preparation for the museum that Hitler planned to build on this site, 'The Exotic Museum of an Extinct Race'. The entrance fee for the Jewish Museum gives you access to six other historic sites – the Klausen, Maisel, Pinkas and Spanish

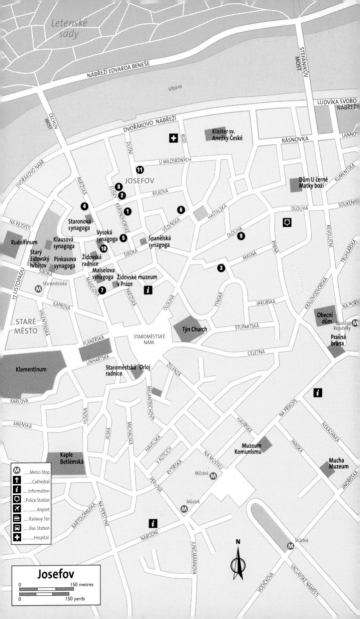

synagogues, the Old Jewish Cemetery and the Ceremonial Hall –
and the Robert Gutmann Gallery. The ticket can be bought at any
one of these sites. Men are required to cover their heads with the
paper hats provided. Women do not need to wear any type of head
cover. ⓐ U Staré školy 1 ⓣ 221 711 511 ⓦ www.jewishmuseum.cz
ⓛ 09.00–18.00 (summer); 09.00–16.30 (winter); closed Sat &
Jewish holidays

Klausová synagoga (Klausen Synagogue)

Rising from the ashes of the fire that devastated Josefov in 1689,
Klausen Synagogue was rebuilt in 1694. The largest of the six
synagogues in the Jewish ghetto, Klausen was the home of the
Jewish Burial Society in Prague. A permanent exhibit, entitled
'Jewish Customs and Traditions', shows everyday life in the Jewish
community and customs connected with birth, circumcision, *bar
mitzvah*, weddings, divorce and the Jewish household. The second
half of this exhibit is located in the Ceremonial Hall next door.
ⓐ U Stareho hrbitova 1

Maiselova synagoga (Maisel Synagogue)

Housing a fascinating collection of Jewish silver, textiles, prints
and books, most of them brought to Prague by the Nazis, Maisel
Synagogue is named after Mordechai Maisel, the mayor of
Prague's Jewish Quarter, who funded the extensive Renaissance
reconstruction of the ghetto. It is currently used as an exhibition
venue and depository. ⓐ Maiselova 10

Pinkasova synagoga (Pinkas Synagogue)

Founded in 1479, Pinkas Synagogue was first turned into a
memorial to the Czech Holocaust victims in 1958. Ten years

later, the Communist government closed the memorial and removed the names from the wall. The names were rewritten on the wall after the fall of Communism in 1989. There is a collection

◆ *Prague's Jewish Museum*

here of paintings and drawings done by children held in the
Czechoslovakian Terezín concentration camp during World War II.
🅐 Široká 3

Španělská synagoga (Spanish Synagogue)

This neo-Moorish structure was built in 1868. It is a beautiful
building inside and out, with a domed ceiling, Islamic motifs and
stained glass. Restored in 1998, the synagogue houses an exhibition
on the history of Czech Jews. 🅐 Dušní 12

Staronová synagoga (Old-New Synagogue)

Of all the synagogues in Prague, this is perhaps the most important.
It has stood here since the 13th century, and despite fires, floods and
the Nazi occupation, it remains the functional, spiritual centre of
the Jewish community today. Built around 1270 by Christian
architects (as Jews could not be architects), the Old-New Synagogue
is the oldest working synagogue in Europe and one of Prague's
earliest Gothic buildings. As in all Orthodox synagogues, the men
and women are segregated and only the men are allowed in the
main hall. This is a single-storey building, so the women's galley is
not upstairs, as is customary. Instead, there are side corridors where
the women stand to view the services through narrow slits in the
wall. Franz Kafka's *bar mitzvah* was held here. On the west wall of
the main hall, there is a glass case shaped like the two stone tablets
on which Moses chiselled the Ten Commandments. Tiny light bulbs
fill the case, lighting up on the anniversary of someone's death; one
of the lights is for Franz Kafka. 🅐 Červená 2 🅛 09.00–16.30
Mon–Thur, 09.00–14.00 Fri, closed Sat

Starý židovský hřbitov (Old Jewish Cemetery)

One of the most impressive sights in the Jewish Quarter is the Old Jewish Cemetery. It was used from 1439 to 1787 and is the oldest existing Jewish cemetery in Europe. The Nazis made it a policy to destroy Jewish cemeteries, sometimes using the tombstones for target practice, but Hitler ordered that this cemetery be left intact. There are more than 100,000 Jews buried in this small plot; the graves are layered 12 deep in some places. The graves stand crowded and askew, decorated with small pebbles placed by visitors, as is the custom. The most prominent graves are those of Mordechai Maisel, a leader of the Prague Jewish community in the 1600s, and Rabbi Loew, the mystical Rabbi who summoned forth the Golem (see page 93). ⓐ Široká 2, entrance from Pinkas Synagogue

🔺 *Josefov's Old Jewish Cemetery is an atmospheric and beautiful place*

Vysoká synagoga (High Synagogue)

Founded by Mordechai Maisel, the mayor of Prague's Jewish Quarter, the High Synagogue is no longer open to the public for tours. It was named for the lofty position of its prayer room located on the second floor of the building. It now functions as a non-Orthodox synagogue. ⓐ Červená 4

Židovská radnice (Jewish Town Hall)

An 18th-century Rococo building, the Jewish Town Hall is the centre of Prague's Jewish community today. Note the clock on the façade with Hebrew numbers; the hands turn counter-clockwise, because Hebrew reads from right to left. ⓐ Červená 2

RETAIL THERAPY

Pařížská, named after the city of Paris, is the Jewish quarter's main thoroughfare and is now the swankiest shopping section in town, being home to Louis Vuitton, Hermès, Francesca Biasia, and the Czech home accessories store, Le Patio. Nearby, on the streets Dlouhá, Dušní and V Kolkovně, is emerging as a fashion district, attracting some of the country's best-known designers, including Bohéme, Klára Nademlýnská, Tatiana and Timoure et Group. All these shops are close to the Staroměstská metro station.

Bohéme An affordable, modern Czech clothing store for women with particularly good sweaters and leather jackets. ⓐ Dušní 8, Prague 1 ⓣ 224 813 840 ⓦ www.boheme.cz ⓛ 11.00–20.00 Mon–Fri, 11.00–17.00 Sat

▶ *Top shopping on Pařížská*

Chez Parisienne Gives you a glimpse of what the high-powered executives and local diplomats wear under their clothes.
ⓐ Pařížská 8 ① 224 817 786 🕐 11.00–18.00 Mon–Sat

Francesco Biasia She's known for her fur purses and buttery leather goods. Storekeepers boast that their business is 90 per cent Czech, which ensures that what you buy will be a unique piece back home.
ⓐ Pařížská 5 ① 224 812 700 🕐 11.00–18.00 Mon–Sat

Hermès Stocking a colourful array of Hermès' iconic ties and scarves, there are also a few other fashion gems that break away from the typical Hermès line. ⓐ Pařížská 12 ① 224 817 545 ⓦ www.hermes.com
🕐 11.00–18.00 Mon–Sat

Klára Nademlýnská One of the Czech Republic's best-known young designers, Klára ensures hot haute fashion in the best-looking boutique in town. ⓐ Dlouhá 3 ① 224 188 769 ⓦ www.klaranademlynska.cz
🕐 10.00–19.00 Mon–Fri, 11.00–18.00 Sat & Sun

Lapin House Prague's hippest children's clothing shop for debutots sells sundry items for princesses, as well as a smaller selection of denim clothes for princes. ⓐ Pařížská 3 ① 224 236 525

Louis Vuitton This Prague shop stocks the full line of trademark beige-and-brown LV handbags and other luxurious accessories.
ⓐ Pařížská 11 ① 224 812 774 🕐 10.00–18.00 Mon–Fri

Sejto Gorgeous hand- and silk-printed textiles are to be had in this unique home store. ⓐ Dlouhá 24 ① 222 320 370 ⓦ www.sejto.cz
🕐 10.00–19.00 Mon–Fri, 11.00–16.00 Sat

Tatiana Tatiana Kovaříková creates beautiful women's clothes. It's definitely worth poking around this shop to see what's in store, from corsets to zip-up capes. ⓐ Dušní 1 ⓣ 224 813 723 ⓦ www.tatiana.cz ⓛ 10.00–19.00 Mon–Fri, 11.00–16.00 Sat

Timoure et Group A pair of Czech designers who create well-tailored coats, suits, trousers, jackets and sweaters, with a dash of inspiration. ⓐ V Kolkovně 6 ⓣ 222 327 358 ⓦ www.timoure.cz

TAKING A BREAK

Bakery Mansson £ ❶ This bakery is so good, they baked the cake for Mick Jagger's 60th birthday party celebration. Simple interior, with only a few café tables and a long counter that boasts a delicious selection of breads and cakes. Healthy breakfasts are served, and lunches mean home-made rye bread sandwiches stuffed with all kinds of fillings, and there are salads too. ⓐ Bílkova 8 ⓣ 222 310 620 ⓝ Metro: Staroměstská or Náměstí Republiky

Potrefená husa £ ❷ This is part of a modern, brewery-owned chain, their menu is straightforward, the beer is tasty and service is usually very good (sadly uncommon in these parts). ⓐ Bílkova 5 ⓣ 222 326 626 ⓝ Metro: Staroměstská, then Tram: 17 or 53 to Právnická fakulta

Siva £ ❸ Arabian-style tea and coffee room with water pipes, pillows, low tables and laid-back music. An oasis in the middle of Prague. ⓐ Masná 8 ⓣ 222 315 983 ⓦ www.cajiky.cz ⓛ 12.00–24.00 ⓝ Metro: Náměstí Republiky

Valmont £ ❹ A window-wrapped Continental café that's a good place for lunch or an afternoon drink. The restaurant is perfect in warm weather, when rattan chairs and tables tumble onto the pavement. The steaks are excellent. ⓐ Pařížská 19 ⓣ 222 327 260 ⓜ Metro: Staroměstská

Velký Blondýn £ ❺ This new café is a great place to people-watch, with large windows and a steady flow of espresso or beer. Evenings can turn into film screenings, if everyone's in the mood. ⓐ Elišky Krásnohorské 12 ⓣ 222 326 651 ⓛ 09.00–22.00 Mon–Fri, 12.00–01.00 Sat ⓜ Metro: Staroměstská

AFTER DARK

Restaurants
Česká hospoda £ ❻ The potato pancake pizzas are out of this world. Good international selection of food, and great beer on tap. ⓐ Vězeňská 9 ⓣ 222 317 330 ⓦ www.ceskahospoda.cz ⓛ 10.00–23.00 ⓜ Metro: Staroměstská

U Golema £ ❼ Dark furniture, walls and ceiling and even monstrous service all seem to be in keeping with the Golem theme. Local and international dishes are on offer as well as excellent Moravian wines. ⓐ Maiselova 8 ⓣ 222 328 165 ⓛ 10.00–23.00 ⓜ Metro: Staroměstská

Café La Veranda ££ ❽ Offers 'fusion light' specialities in a modern setting. For a special occasion, try the 'sexy menu', a combination of five of the best entrées. ⓐ Elišky Krásnohorské 2/10 ⓣ 224 814 733 ⓛ 12.00–24.00 ⓦ www.laveranda.cz ⓜ Metro: Staroměstská

Láry Fáry ££ **9** Design-heavy place with good sound, excellent location and an extensive menu of dishes. Try the skewered meats. Good first date pick. **ⓐ** Dlouhá 30 **ⓣ** 222 320 154 **ⓦ** www.laryfary.cz **🕐** 11.00–23.00 **Ⓜ** Metro: Náměstí Republiky

Restaurace Pravda ££ **10** Situated beside the Old-New Synagogue, this stylish space offers risky global fusion and caters to vegetarians and meat-eaters alike. Cool lighting, comfortable seating and helpful staff. **ⓐ** Pařížská 17 **ⓣ** 222 326 203 **Ⓜ** Metro: Staroměstská

⬤ *Josefov has lots of in places to eat out*

Isabella £££ ⑪ A skilled chef and the cosy environs of the Bellagio Hotel make this the perfect place for popping the question or at least making a pricey proposition. ⓐ U milosrdných 2 ⓣ 224 819 957 ⓜ Metro: Staroměstská

Bars, clubs & theatres

NoD No, nobody sleeps here. NoD is a multifunctional space in the centre of Prague which contains a theatre, gallery, media lab, cinema, presentation hall and café. ⓐ above the Roxy on Dlouhá 33 ⓣ 224 826 330 ⓦ www.roxy.cz ⓛ 13.00–23.00 ⓜ Metro: Náměstí Republiky, then Tram: 8 or 14 to Dlouhá třída

Aloha Wave Lounge Cool fun in summer and a hot spot in winter. A wood interior and dimmed lights provide for a relaxed ambience while you watch surfing films on the wide screen, sip exotic cocktails or toss back some Pacific cuisine. Live DJs and bands play regularly. ⓐ Dušní 11 ⓣ 724 055 704 ⓛ café 08.30–02.00, cocktail lounge 18.00–02.00, both open until 04.00 Wed–Sat ⓜ Metro: Staroměstská

Confessions Friendly owner/managers make Confessions a relaxing and sociable night out, a welcome respite from Old Town prices too. Two rooms with DJs, drink specials, funky tunes and fussball – this is a chilled-out winner. ⓐ U milosrdných 4 ⓛ 16.00–03.00 Mon–Fri, 17.00–02.00 Sat ⓜ Metro: Staroměstská

THE GOLEM

Throughout Prague you may see items with the word 'Golem' on them. These relate to Jewish Prague's version of the Frankenstein monster. Golem originally meant 'embryo' or 'imperfect matter', though it is now a Hebrew and Yiddish slang term for a thick-skulled person.

The story begins during the reign of Emperor Rudolf II in the 17th century. The emperor was indifferent to the church, and entertained alchemists, artists, astronomers and mystics at court. He befriended Rabbi Loew, a well-known Jewish scholar who was expert in interpreting the Cabbala. Rabbi Loew became a favoured 'Court Jew', frequently able to intercede on behalf of Jews who were being routinely persecuted at that time.

As alchemists try to make gold out of base metals, cabbalists work on ways of animating simple matter. Rabbi Loew took a ball of clay from the Vltava River, formed a figure out of it, placed in its mouth a *shem*, or charm, and the Golem came to life. The Rabbi ordered the Golem to protect the Jewish Quarter from attack. But the monster had a mind of its own.

Legend has it that the Golem finally ran amok and the Rabbi had to interrupt his Sabbath service in the Synagogue to deal with it. His congregation kept repeating the verse in a psalm that they had been reciting until the Rabbi returned. To commemorate this event, a line repeats in the Sabbath service at the Old-New Synagogue to this day. The end of the Golem came when the Rabbi removed the *shem* from its mouth and carried its lifeless remains to the attic of the Old-New Synagogue where, legend has it, they reside to this day.

Malá Strana & Hradčany

Hradčany is where the Prague Castle lords over Prague. The ascent on foot, tram or metro provides you with many sublime views of the city, its grandeur laid out before you in all directions. The cliff-top site is certainly fit for a monarch, and the castle complex itself is rich in architectural gems.

The Malá Strana (Lesser Quarter) is anything but diminutive. This storybook-beautiful area was founded in the 13th century by merchants who set up shop at the base of the castle. Traced with narrow, winding lanes boasting palaces and red-roofed burgher houses, Malá Strana is filled with pricier pubs and restaurants, quirky boutiques and foreign embassies. If you feel a sense of déjà vu, it's because the area has played a prominent part in many Czech and foreign films. If you are lucky enough to be able to linger here for a while, you may be asked to appear as an extra.

SIGHTS & ATTRACTIONS

Chrám sv. Mikuláše (St Nicolas Church)
This church is one of the most valuable buildings of the 'Prague Baroque' period, complete with dominant dome and belfry. The inside decoration of the church is a glorious example of High Baroque style. Mozart played the organ here during his stay in Prague. ❸ Malostranské nám. 25 ❶ 257 534 215 ❶ 09.00–16.00, concerts often start at 17.00 Ⓜ Metro: Malostranská

Karlův most (Charles Bridge)
Dating from 1357, one of Prague's foremost attractions links Prague Castle and the Malá Strana to Staré Město. Built to replace the

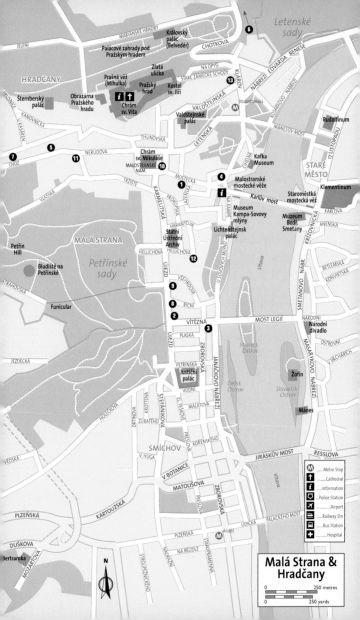

Malá Strana & Hradčany

MARIÁNSKÉ HRADBY

JELENÍ

Palácové zahrady pod
Pražským hradem

Královský
palác
(Belvedér)

CHOTKOVA

NA OPYŠI

Letenské
sady

6

KLÁROV

NÁBŘEŽÍ EDVARDA BENEŠE

HRADČANY

Prašná věž
(Mihulka)

Zlatá
ulička

Pražský
hrad

STARÉ ZÁMECKÉ SCHODY

13

Šternberský
palác

Obrazárna
Pražského
hradu

Chrám
sv. Víta

Kostel
sv. Jiří

Malostranská

M

Rudolfinum

17. LISTOPADU

KANOVNICKÁ

U KASÁREN

VALDŠTEJNSKÁ

Valdštejnský
palác

MÁNESŮV MOST

MÁNESŮV MOST

KOLKOVNÁ

STARÉ
MĚSTO

THUNOVSKÁ

Klementinum

5

NERUDOVA

Chrám
sv. Mikuláše

LETENSKÁ

CIHELNÁ

Kafka
Museum

7

11

MALOSTRANSKÉ
NÁM.

10

Karlova most

Staroměstská
mostecká věž

KARLOVA

U ÚVOZ

UVOZ

MOSTECKÁ

1

4

Malostranské
mostecké věže

i

KŘIŽOVNICKÁ

ANENSKÁ

VLAŠSKÁ

TRŽIŠTĚ

KARMELITSKÁ

PROKOPSKÁ

Museum
Kampa-Sovovy
mlýny

Muzeum
Bedř.
Smetany

HAŠTALSKÁ

MALÁ STRANA

HARANTOVA

NA KAMPĚ

BETLÉMSKÁ

Petřín
Hill

Petřínské
sady

Státní
Ústřední
Archiv

HELLICHOVA

Lichtenštejnský
palác

Vltava

KONVIKTSKÁ

SMETANOVO NÁBŘ.

NÁRODNÍ

Bludiště na
Petřínské

12

OSTROVNÍ

STRAHOVSKÁ

VŠEHRDOVA

ÚJEZD

Národní
divadlo

Funicular

9

ŘÍČNÍ

8

VÍTĚZNÁ

MOST LEGIÍ

MASARYKOVO NÁBŘEŽÍ

JIRCHÁŘÍCH

JEZDECKÁ

2

3

Střelecký
Ostrov

ÚJEZD

PLASKÁ

ZBOROVSKÁ

JANÁČKOVO NÁBŘEŽÍ

Dětský
Ostrov

Žofín

PETŘINSKÁ

Slovanský
Ostrov

Justiční
palác

ŠTEFÁNIKOVA

VODNÍ

MALÁTOVA

Máches

HOLEČKOVA

 OSTROVNÍHO

ZUBATÉHO

PLZEŇSKÁ

KŘÍŽOVÁ

SMÍCHOV

PRESLOVA

KOŘENSKÉHO

V HUGA

JIRÁSKŮV MOST

RESSLOVA

VEDSKÁ

V BOTANICE

MATOUŠOVA

ZBOROVSKÁ

PRESLOVA

Vltava

LÍDICKÁ

PLZEŇSKÁ

KARTOUZSKÁ

DUŠKOVA

PLZEŇSKÁ

NA BĚLIDLE

STAROPRAMENNÁ

Anděl

M

LÍDICKÁ

PALACKÉHO MOST

Bertramka

MOZARTOVA

ŠTEFÁNIKOVA

NÁDRAŽNÍ

STŘÍBRNÉHO

N

Malá Strana &
Hradčany

0 ————— 250 metres

0 ————— 250 yards

earlier, 12th-century Judith's Bridge, this half-kilometre ($^1/_4$-mile) span has survived floods and acted as Prague's main pedestrian promenade across the Vltava River for nearly 600 years. Today, the bridge hosts a busy mix of tourists, locals, artists and busking minstrels. The best time to stroll across the bridge is early morning and around sunset, when the crowds have thinned and lamplight casts mysterious shadows on the 30 hulking statues along its edge. The oldest of these portrays Jan of Nepomuk, the most popular national saint of Bohemia, supposedly martyred by King Wenceslas for refusing to divulge the confessional secrets of the king's wife, who was cheating on her husband. The newest of the statues depicts Cyril and Methodius, brothers born in the Byzantine Empire in the 9th century who became Christian missionaries to the Slavic peoples. The statues are all copies, the valuable originals being housed in the Lapidarium of the National Gallery.

Malostranské mostecké věže (Lesser Town Bridge Towers)

Located at the western end of Charles Bridge, the smaller tower is the remaining relic of Judith Bridge, a Romanesque bridge constructed in the 12th century and destroyed by flood in 1342. The taller tower was designed to match the Old Town Bridge Tower. The permanent exhibition within this tower on the history of Charles Bridge is worth a visit. ☎ 257 530 487 ⏰ 10.00–18.00 (summer only), admission charged Ⓜ Metro: Malostranská

Staroměstská mostecká věž (Old Town Bridge Tower)

The bridge tower on the Old Town side of Charles Bridge was built at the same time as the Gothic bridge itself. It was built not only as a fortified tower but also as a symbolic triumphal arch on the Bohemian kings' coronation route, a fact to which the richly sculptured decorations on its eastern façade clearly attest. Inside the tower is an exhibition of old musical instruments from the National Museum collections. ☎ 224 220 569 🕐 10.00–18.00 Mar, 10.00–19.00 Apr–May, 10.00–22.00 June–Sept, 10.00–19.00 Oct, 10.00–17.00 Nov–Feb

🔺 *Let Malá Strana dawn on you*

Palácové zahrady pod Pražským hradem (Palatial Gardens below Prague Castle)

Situated on the southern slopes of the castle you'll find beautiful views of Malá Strana among the fussy terraces, monumental staircases and fountains of these truly palatial gardens.
ⓐ Valdštejnské náměstí 3 ⓣ 257 010 401 ⓛ 10.00–18.00 (summer), small admission charged ⓜ Metro: Malostranská

Petřín Hill

Ride the funicular to the top of this hill to find a miniature Eiffel Tower that functioned as the city's primary telecommunications tower until the Žižkov TV Tower opened across town. Those who climb the 59 m (195 ft) will be treated to striking views, day or night. Just hanging around in the gardens is fun. Bring a Frisbee and some local red wine, and make an afternoon of it. Another enjoyable diversion is the Bludiště na Petříně, a mirror maze with a depiction of Prague students fighting against Swedes on the Charles Bridge in 1648. ⓣ 257 315 212 ⓛ 10.00–19.00, closed Mon in winter, small admission charged ⓜ Tram: 12, 22, or 23 to Újezd, then ride the funicular to the top

Pražský hrad (Prague Castle)

According to the *Guinness World Records*, Prague Castle is the largest ancient castle in the world. The huge hill-top complex on Hradčanské náměstí includes dozens of architectural monuments that provide some of the best views of town. The top sights in the complex are St Vitus Cathedral, the Royal Palace, St George's Basilica, Mihulka Powder Tower and Golden Lane. It costs nothing to walk around the complex, so you can explore the hulking exterior of the castle and enjoy the beauty of all the buildings even if you're tight on cash. It's a lovely place to wander around after dark as well, as it's generally lit until midnight. If you do want to go into the museums and buildings, buy tickets at the Prague Castle Information Centre in the second courtyard after you pass through the main gate from Hradčanské náměstí. Tickets for the five main attractions are your best bargain at 350 Kč (520 Kč for families). ❸ Hradčanské nám. ❶ 224 373 368 ❷ ticket office 09.00–17.00 ❾ www.hrad.cz ❿ Metro: Malostranská or Hradčanská, then Tram: 22 or 23 to Hradčanské náměstí

Chrám sv. Víta (St Vitus Cathedral) was built in the year 926 as the court church of the Přemyslid princes and has since been the site for the coronation of Prague's kings and queens as well as the final resting place for royalty. The key parts of its Gothic construction were built in the 14th century, and the 18th and 19th centuries produced subsequent Baroque and Neo-Gothic additions. As you enter the cathedral through the back entrance into the main aisle, you'll notice the two central stained-glass windows, which depict the Holy Trinity, with the Virgin Mary to the left and Sv. Václav (St Wenceslas) kneeling to the right. The most interesting window in the cathedral was designed by the famous Czech art nouveau artist, Alfons Mucha. Of the massive Gothic cathedral's 21 chapels, the **Svatováclavská kaple (St Wenceslas Chapel)** is the most impressive. Encrusted with hundreds of pieces of jasper and amethyst and decorated with paintings from the 14th to the 16th centuries, this chapel houses the crown jewels and the tomb of Bohemia's patron saint, St Wenceslas. Just beyond this, the **Kaple sv. Kříže (Chapel of the Holy Rood)** leads to the entrance of the underground royal crypt where newly restored sarcophagi hold the remains of kings and their relatives. The centre sarcophagus is the final resting place of Karel IV (Charles IV), the Bohemian king who ruled during Prague's 'Golden Age'. In the back row are Charles's four wives (all placed in one sarcophagus), and in front of them is Jiří z Poděbrad (George of Poděbrady), the last king of Bohemia, who died in 1471.

○ *Zlatá ulička in the castle precincts*

Královský palác (Royal Palace) is where Bohemian kings and princes resided from the 9th century, and the vaulted **Vladislavský sál (Vladislav Hall)**, once used for the coronation of kings, is now used for special occasions of state such as inaugurations of presidents and state visits.

Kostel sv. Jiří (St George's Basilica), adjacent to the Royal Palace, is Prague's oldest Romanesque structure, dating from the 10th century. It also houses Bohemia's first convent. No longer serving a religious function, the convent now contains relics of the castle's history and a gallery of Gothic Czech art.

Zlatá ulička (Golden Lane) is a chocolate-box row of tiny 16th-century houses built into the castle fortifications. Once home to castle sharp-shooters and artisans, the houses now contain small shops, galleries, snack bars, and boundless photo opportunities. Franz Kafka lived briefly at number 22.

Obrazárna Pražského hradu (Prague Castle Picture Gallery) displays European and Bohemian masterpieces. The most celebrated is Hans von Aachen's *Portrait of a Girl* (1605–10), depicting the artist's daughter.

Prašná věž (Mihulka Powder Tower) forms part of the northern bastion of the castle complex just off Golden Lane. Built as a defence tower in the late 15th century, it became a forger's workshop, where cannons and bells were made. It was turned into a laboratory for the 17th-century alchemists serving Emperor Rudolf II, and later became a gunpowder store. It is now a museum of alchemy, forging and Renaissance castle life.

CULTURE

MOZART AND PRAGUE

In the late 18th century, Prague was a city to rival all others in Europe. After surviving a devastating fire, the city burst into a frenzy of renovation and redesign influenced by rich German, Spanish and Italian noblemen. They left their mark with incredible Baroque-style palaces, churches and gardens. The city's population grew to 100,000, and as the economic situation improved, the stage was set for artistic inspiration.

A Viennese Wunderkind named Wolfgang Amadeus Mozart waltzed into Prague just as this artistic explosion was at its height, and found here a skilled orchestra and an appreciative audience. He moved into a beautiful villa named **Bertramka**, to concentrate on his *magnum opus*. In the beautiful gardens and Baroque drawing rooms he found inspiration and wrote one of his most famous operas. In 1787, the Estates Theatre in Prague staged its premiere, and the world fell in love with *Don Giovanni*.

As a result, on almost any day of the week you will find some venue paying tribute to Mozart, one of Prague's most famous adopted sons. It is worth attending at least one performance; Czech musicians are some of the best, the price is about half of what you'd pay in other European venues, and even if you don't care for the music, you will not fail to be inspired by the surroundings.

Admission is charged for all of the following:

Bertramka This former residence of Mozart is now a permanent exhibition dedicated to the life and work of the great composer. Mozartova 169 257 318 461 09.00–18.00 (summer); 09.30–16.00 (winter) www.bertramka.com Metro: Anděl, then Tram: 4, 7, 9 or 10 to Bertramka

Kafka Museum The life and work of Franz Kafka is displayed in photographs, manuscripts, diaries, correspondence and first editions of Kafka's works, as well as audio-visual programmes. Cihelná 2b 221 451 333 10.00–18.00 www.kafkamuseum.cz Metro: Malostranská

Museum Kampa-Sovovy mlýny Once a mill, this newly renovated museum displays beautiful collections of famous Czech and central European artists, such as Kupka and Gutfreund. U Sovových mlýnů 503/2 257 286 147 10.00–18.00 www.museumkampa.cz Metro: Malostranská

Šternberský palác (Šternberk Palace) Adjacent to the main gate of Prague Castle, this gallery is also known as the European Art Museum, as it displays an eclectic range of European art spanning five centuries, from Orthodox iconography to works by Rembrandt, El Greco, Goya and Van Dyck. If you have time for only one museum during your stay, this is a good choice. Hradčanské nám. 15 233 090 570 www.ngprague.cz 10.00–18.00 Tues–Sun Metro: Malostranská or Hradčanská

RETAIL THERAPY

Capriccio The shop for noteworthy sheet music. Újezd 15 257 320 165 10.00–17.00 Mon–Sat Tram: Újezd

La Perla Art Features sheer silks from India; the owner selects only the most interesting designs. Malostranské náměstí 11 257 531 628 10.00–18.00 Metro: Malostranská

Material Glass shop with unique up-market pieces you can't find anywhere else. U Lužického semináře 7 257 533 663 10.00–18.00 Metro: Malostranská

Nostalgie Antique Specialising in old textiles and jewellery, most of the textiles here are pre-World War II. Jánský Vršek 8 257 530 049 10.00–18.00 Mon–Fri Metro: Malostranská

Nový Smíchov A modern, sleek shopping mall that has everything for every taste. A great place and convenient location for rainy-day window shopping. Plzeňská 8 251 101 061 09.00–21.00 Metro: Anděl

Obchod Pod lampou Handmade, one-of-a-kind marionettes that deserve to become family treasures. U Lužického semináře 5 606 924 392 www.loutky.com 10.00–18.00 Metro: Malostranská

◀ *Picture-perfect Charles Bridge*

Little Shop Romen A unique shop focusing on Romany culture. Inside you'll find a comprehensive selection of Romany music and books, as well as some very good and unusual folk art, like pictures made from broken glass, kitchen utensils carved from a single piece of wood, and traditional dolls made from wooden spoons.
ⓐ Nerudova 32 ⓣ 257 532 800 ⓛ 10.00–18.00 Mon–Sat ⓜ Metro: Malostranská

Shakespeare & Sons Thousands of hand-picked new and used English titles are to be found in this extensive bookshop.
ⓐ U Lužického semináře 10 ⓣ 257 531 894 ⓦ www.shakes.cz
ⓛ 11.00–21.00 ⓜ Metro: Malostranská

TAKING A BREAK

Bakeshop Diner £ ❶ Massive gourmet sandwiches, fantastic baked goods and salads all within an easy walk to Charles Bridge.
ⓐ Lázeňská 19 ⓣ 257 534 244 ⓦ www.bakeshop.cz ⓛ 07.00–19.00
ⓜ Metro: Malostranská

Bohemia Bagel £ ❷ This place is always full, and the bottomless cups of coffee are a refreshing treat. Bagels with all the trimmings will keep you going all day. ⓐ Újezd 16 ⓣ 257 310 694
ⓦ www.bohemiabagel.cz ⓛ 07.00–24.00 ⓜ Tram: 22 or 23 to Újezd

Café Savoy £ ❸ Fabulously French, with Edith Piaf resonating against the Neo-Renaissance ceiling. Home-made pastries and cakes and foreign-language newspapers make this one of the nicest nooks in town. ⓐ Vítězná 5 ⓣ 257 311 562 ⓛ 08.00–22.30 Mon–Fri, 09.00–22.30 Sat & Sun ⓜ Tram: 22 or 23 to Újezd

Kafíčko £ ❹ Serves great coffee and teas in quiet, smoke-free surroundings just a street away from tourist mayhem. Let the world churn itself into a frenzy while you take the cake. ⓐ Míšeňská 10 ❶ 724 151 795 ⏱ 10.00–22.00 Ⓜ Metro: Malostranská

U Zavěšenýho Kafe £ ❺ 'At the Hanging Coffee' has long been associated with Czech artists, musicians and intellectuals who frequent the place. 'Hanging a coffee' is local vernacular for purchasing a coffee in advance for somebody who has yet to arrive. Hang out here for the coffee and for choice morsels like satay with peanut sauce, roast duck with cherry sauce, or traditional pickled Hermelín (Czech Camembert). ⓐ Úvoz 6 ❶ 257 532 868 ⏱ 10.00–24.00 Ⓜ Metro: Hradčanská, then Tram: 22 or 23 to Pohořelec

AFTER DARK

Restaurants
Haveli £ ❻ Authentic Indian in a beautiful cellar restaurant under vaulted ceilings with a good selection of vegetarian offerings. ⓐ Dejvická 6 ❶ 233 34 48 00 ⓦ www.haveli.cz ⏱ 11.00–23.00 Ⓜ Metro: Hradčanská

Malý Buddha £ ❼ Intimate and non-smoking Asian eatery in an easy-to-miss location as you're walking from the castle. Do yourself a favour and don't miss it. ⓐ Úvoz 46 ❶ 220 513 894 ⏱ 13.00–22.30 Tues–Sun Ⓜ Metro: Hradčanská, then Tram: 22 or 23 to Pohořelec

Olympia ££ ❽ Serves great Czech food up until midnight in the atmosphere of a 1930s Czech watering hole where you'll find Pilsner

Urquell on tap. ⓐ Vítěžová 7 ⓣ 251 511 080 Ⓝ Metro: Malostranská or
Narodníi Divadlo, then Tram: 22 or 23 to Újezd

Restaurant La Bastille ££ ❾ A laid-back French restaurant with
excellent food and atmosphere. Lamb, pork, fish, mussels and frogs'
legs are all served with flair. ⓐ Újezd 26/426 ⓣ 257 312 830
Ⓦ www.labastille.cz ⓛ 12.00–01.00 Ⓝ Tram: 22 or 23 to Újezd

⬤ *Malá Strana serves it up with style*

Square ££ ❿ Serves up trend-setting cocktails, coffee, tapas, breakfast and primarily Italian cuisine with impeccable atmosphere. The wine list, food, good service and great location are a rarity. ⓐ Malostranské nám. 5 ⓣ 257 532 109 ⓛ 08.00–01.00 ⓦ www.squarerestaurant.cz ⓜ Metro: Malostranská, then Tram: 22 or 23 to Malostranské nám.

U Sedmi švábů ££ ⓫ 'At the Seven Cockroaches' is a medieval experience complete with cellar dining, fire-eating, duelling and even torture as entertainment. Traditional recipes use only authentic 15th- and 16th-century ingredients, so no tomatoes or potatoes. ⓐ Jánský vršek 14 ⓣ 257 531 455 ⓛ 11.00–23.00 ⓜ Metro: Malostranská, then Tram: 22 or 23 to Malostranské nám.

Alchymist £££ ⓬ Fabulous décor and service and a menu that serves up choice foie gras, sea bass, lamb and divine desserts. Expensive wines might mean exercising the credit card. ⓐ Hellichova 4 ⓣ 257 312 518 ⓦ www.alchymist.cz ⓜ Metro: Malostranská, then Tram: 22 or 23 to Hellichova

Palffy Palace £££ ⓭ The ambience of this antique, turn-of-the-century dining room is shabby chic, and a must for those wanting to have an upscale Central European dining experience. Views of the castle gardens are free. ⓐ Valdštejnská 14 ⓣ 257 530 522 ⓛ 11.00–23.00 ⓜ Metro: Malostranská

Bars & clubs
JJ Murphy's They have Guinness, so belly up to this Irish bar, or get a couch-potato view of live sport in the attic lounge room. Proper

breakfasts and hamburgers served. ⓐ Tržiště 4 ⓣ 257 535 575
ⓦ www.jjmurphys.cz ⓛ 10.00–01.00 ⓝ Metro: Malostranská, then
Tram: 22 or 23 to Malostranské nám.

Klub Lávka A firm Prague favourite, 'Club Avalanche' facilities
include five themed dancing rooms, a café, restaurant, and many
themed bars on different levels. The tequila bar is a direct hit.
ⓐ Novotného lávka ⓣ 221 082 299 ⓛ 21.30–05.00 ⓝ Metro:
Malostranská

Malostranská Beseda 'The Meeting House' has an incredible
location on Malá Strana Square, blasting beats towards embassies
and state offices across the way. Live music happens in this two-
room bar almost every night of the week, usually jazz-flavoured
rock. ⓐ Malostranské nám. 21 ⓣ 257 532 092 ⓝ Metro: Malostranská;
Tram: 20 or 22 to Malostranské nám.

St Nicolas Wine Bar This place has attracted dedicated drinkers of all
vogues for years. The jazzy vibe lasts until the other side of
midnight, and bar snacks help you stay the distance. ⓐ Tržiště 10
ⓛ 12.00–01.00 Mon–Fri, 16.00–01.00 Sat & Sun ⓝ Metro:
Malostranská, then Tram: 22 or 23 to Malostranské nám.

U Černého Vola 'At the Black Bull' is situated right by the castle. One
of the best and cheapest pubs in the area, known for its excellent
dark beer, but not for food. You know it's time to leave when they
throw you out. ⓐ Loretánské náměstí 1 ⓣ 220 513 481
ⓛ 09.00–22.00 ⓝ Metro: Hradčanská, then Tram: 22 or 23 to
Brušnice

Újezd Young punks love the shabby, anarchistic cellar décor, the live music and the DJs. Upstairs is a more chilled-out experience. Either way, it's going to be a late night. ⓐ Újezd 18 ⓣ 257 316 537 ⓛ 11.00–04.00 Ⓝ Tram: 22 or 23 to Újezd

U Malého Glena 'At Little Glen's' has been serving up strong coffee and cool jazz on Prague's Left Bank for a long time. Thankfully, they're still going strong, so you can see live bands almost every night, or at least sit and chat in this friendly jazz cellar/café. ⓐ Karmelitská 23 ⓣ 257 531 717 ⓛ 21.30–00.30 Ⓦ www.malyglen.cz Ⓝ Metro: Malostranská

🔺 *Malá Strana – the Lesser Quarter makes a big impression*

Vinohrady, Vyšehrad & Žižkov

Once upon a time, it was a vineyard. Voted the city's 'best neighbourhood to live in', **Vinohrady** is now a great combination of city-centre amenities, handsome art nouveau apartment buildings, and tourist-free tranquillity, based around Náměstí Míru square. Wenceslas Square is just a short stroll down Vinohradská, but the hustle and bustle of touristville seems a world away. Boasting some excellent neighbourhood cafés, pubs and restaurants, as well as some striking architecture, Vinohrady is sure to please. **Vyšehrad** is the final resting place of some of Prague's most famous artists and is also home to some amazing Czech Cubist architecture. **Žižkov** is Vinohrady's rowdy neighbour on the other side of the tracks. Once an open space where they buried Prague's plague victims, it is now anything but dead. Home to a large Romany (gypsy) population, and historically one of the city's poorer districts, it is now up-and-coming, its counter-culture attracting expat hipsters and party animals from all over the globe.

All three districts developed in an optimistic era in the second half of the 19th century, when Czechoslovakia was trying to shrug off its identity crisis and take pride in its cultural heritage. Among the main attractions of this area are the quiet gardens, plentiful pubs, idiosyncratic clubs, and the strangest-looking TV tower you've ever seen. This proud presentation of neighbourhoods is where you will see how the real Prague lives, and at night, how the real Prague parties.

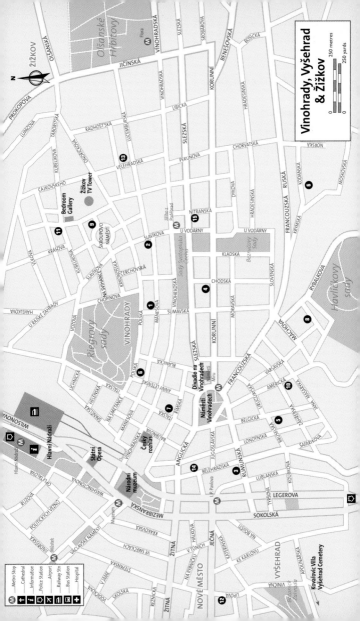

SIGHTS & ATTRACTIONS

Grand tour of Vinohrady architectural styles

Real art nouveau enthusiasts should plan a walk that begins at the Vinohrady Theatre at Náměstí Míru (Peace Square) to see some of Prague's grandest residential streets. Walk down **Římská** and turn right on to **Italská** to see beautiful sculptures, wrought-iron balconies, coloured tiles and glass decorations. At Italská 20, have a look at the house marked 'V Černochově' ('In the Dark Continent'), which features huge lion heads. Take a detour down **Mánesova**, then left along **Slavíkova**, turning left again onto **Polská**, which is quite possibly Prague's prettiest residential street. **Chopinova,** on the right, has some art nouveau and art deco buildings at numbers 4, 6, 8 and 14. Take a right along **Na Švihance**, and nearly every house is a work of art. One street over to the right, **Krkonošská,** has several houses with large sculptures and reliefs, the best one being old father Krakonoš leaning from the corner of **Čerchovská.** Ⓝ Metro: Nam. Miru or Jiřího z Poděbrad

Havlíčkovy sady

Havlíčkovy sady is Prague's second largest park and is located about seven blocks south of Náměstí Míru. Its most notable landmark is the beautiful **Villa Gröbe** (Grébovka), a neo-Renaissance villa built in 1871–88 as a luxury summer house for the industrialist, Moritz Gröbe. This is a perfect place to shake out the picnic blanket and drench yourself in the ambience of the graceful gardens that feature a working, if small, vineyard. Ⓝ Metro: Náměstí Míru, then Tram: 4, 22 or 23 to Ruská and walk about three blocks west to the park entrance

Kovařovic Villa

If you're interested in Czech Cubist architecture, this house is a must-see. Josef Chochol's (1880–1956) architectural creation echoes a Cubist painting. Houses nearby are equally whimsical. To the right is the Modernist Villa Sequens by Otakar Novotný (1912–13), and on the left is a Neo-Classical villa by Emil Kralicek (1912–13). Unfortunately, none of these homes are open to visitors, but they're definitely worth an exterior look. ⓐ Libušina 3 Ⓜ Metro: Vyšehrad

Riegrovy sady

This pleasant park stretches between Italská, Chopinova, Polská and Vozová streets on the northern edge of Vinohrady, at the border with Žižkov. Make your way to the top of the hill and sit on a bench for some fabulous views over the Old Town and Prague Castle. If it's summer, relax and have a beer in the appealing beer garden. You can exit the park at Chopinova, where three more fabulous streets beckon. Ⓜ Metro: Jiřího z Poděbrad

Žižkov TV Tower

Rising like a futuristic spaceship above the working-class quarter of Žižkov, this is one of Prague's most interesting, if controversial, buildings. At 216 m (708 ft), the TV tower is the tallest building in the city, and they say on a clear day you can see it from a full 100 km (60 miles) away. Often regarded as a relic of the Communist era, the tower was actually completed after the Velvet Revolution in 1992. Taking the lift to the top floor affords the visitor some spectacular views of the town, although the cafeteria at the top isn't much to write home about. Artist David Černý's black, computer-inspired babies climbing up the side of the tower lends a bit of whimsy to the structure. On ground level, check out the beautifully haunting

Jewish cemetery leaning off to the side. ⓐ Mahlerovy sady 1 ⓣ 242 418 784 ⓦ www.tower.cz ⓛ 10.00–23.00 Ⓝ Metro: Jiřího z Poděbrad

CULTURE

Bedroom Gallery

This is a non-profit, conceptual art space focusing on all the big isms: feminism, multiculturalism and expatism, to name a few. ⓐ Fibichova 4 ⓣ 603 851 478 ⓛ 14.00–20.00 Thur–Sat Ⓝ Metro: Jiřího z Poděbrad

Divadlo na Vinohradech (Vinohrady Theatre)

This is Vinohrady's grandest art nouveau building, constructed between 1904 and 1907. Statues depicting 'Truth' and 'Bravery' stand on top of the theatre's façade. Catch a ballet performance if you can; the drama is all Czech. ⓐ Náměstí Míru 7 ⓣ 224 257 601 ⓛ box office 11.00–19.00 Mon–Fri, 13.00–16.00 & 16.30–19.00 Sat Ⓝ Metro: Náměstí Míru

Vyšehrad Cemetery

Some of Prague's most famous people rest at the Vyšehrad Cemetery. Open year-round, it's a perfect lookout and diversion from the madness of the city, offering you a calm, shady place to contemplate life. Access is through two gates at either end of the Church of St Peter and St Paul, where you will find a map of the tombs of the most well-known of those buried within. In the centre of the cemetery are individual plots among the beautifully appointed tombs and mausoleums, and at the end of a wide avenue

◀ *Kovařovic Villa – Cubist but not square*

is the Slavín, or Pantheon. Built in 1890, this massive tomb is dedicated to the most honoured figures in the Czech Republic, such as Antonín Dvořák, Alfons Mucha, Jan Neruda and Bedřich Smetana. The family tomb of ex-president Václav Havel is also here.

ⓐ Soběslavova 1 ① 241 410 348 ● 09.30–18.00 (summer); 09.00–16.30 (winter) Ⓝ Metro: Vyšehrad

RETAIL THERAPY

Bazar U Sv. Kateřiny Featuring a fascinating selection of unique antiques, this shop has the ambience of a long-forgotten basement, and low prices to boot. Call first, as they keep irregular hours.
ⓐ Kateřinská 14 ① 224 910 123 Ⓝ Metro: Karlovo Náměstí

Boom Bap Shop Hip-hop record shop in a real, working-class neighbourhood. ⓐ Bělehradská 57 ① 777 319 746 ● 11.00–20.00 Mon–Fri, 12.00–18.00 Sat & Sun Ⓝ Metro: Náměstí Míru

Cellarius Specialist wine shop offering more than 1,000 varieties from around the world; a perfect place to buy something nice to sip in one of the many parks to be found in Vinohrady. ⓐ Budečská 29 ① 222 515 243 ● 10.30–21.00 Mon–Fri, 12.00–21.00 Sat Ⓝ Metro: Náměstí Míru

Palác Flora This relatively new addition to the shopping scene encompasses about 120 reasonably priced shops on four floors, plus a supermarket and an IMAX cinema. The ubiquitous coffee shops are good vantage points from which to watch the local talent.
ⓐ Vinohradská 151 ① 255 741 700 ● 09.00–21.00 Mon–Sat, 10.00–21.00 Sun Ⓝ Metro: Flora

Parthenonas Sells Greek wines, olives and other yummy Greek products. 🅐 Vinohradská 66 📞 724 296 357 🕐 10.00–19.00 Mon–Thur, 10.00–18.00 Fri 🆖 Metro: Jiřího z Poděbrad

Rybanaruby Go with the flow at the 'Inside-out Fish', a multimedia saloon that combines a performance stage, shop and tea house with free internet access. Good used CDs and unique arts and crafts are for sale. 🅐 Manesova 87 🆆 www.rybanaruby.net 🕐 11.00–22.00 Mon–Sat 🆖 Metro: Jiřího z Poděbrad

Shakespeare & Sons Just outside the city centre, S&S offers some excellent reads in a real residential neighbourhood. Kitted out with a comfortable coffee bar up front where you can sit all day, this is the perfect place to review the newest literary finds. At weekends, live bands often play. 🅐 Krymská 12 📞 271 740 839 🆆 www.shakes.cz 🆖 Metro: Náměstí Míru, then Tram: 22 or 23 to Krymská

TAKING A BREAK

Ambiente £ ❶ Located well off the tourist track, Prague's most successful wholly Czech-owned restaurant. Forego pastas in favour of real Argentinian Angus, or tender beef ribs and spicy chicken wings, served up with tangy sauces. 🅐 Mánesova 59 📞 222 727 851 🆆 www.ambi.cz 🕐 11.00–22.00 🆖 Metro: Náměstí Míru

Bio Potraviny – Zdravá Výživa £ ❷ Small health food store on the square. In addition to tofu and soy products, they also sell fresh bread and cookies. 🅐 nám. Jiřího z Poděbrad 5 🕐 09.00–17.00 Mon–Fri 🆖 Metro: Jiřího z Poděbrad

Bohemian Bagel Express £ ❸ Great bagels with all the fillings and coffee at this outdoor stand just a hop, skip and jump from the I.P. Pavlova metro. ⓐ Tylovo náměstí ⓛ 08.00–22.00 Ⓜ Metro: I.P. Pavlova

Dobrá Trafika £ ❹ Good local hangout with a great combination of café, wine shop, tobacconist and newsagent, serving hearty breakfasts and snacks all day long. A smoker's paradise, this place also has outdoor seating for those interested in fresh air. ⓐ Korunní 48 ⓣ 222 510 261 Ⓦ www.dobratrafika.cz ⓛ 07.30–23.00 Mon–Fri, 09.00–23.00 Sat & Sun Ⓜ Metro: Jiřího z Poděbrad

Medúza £ ❺ Cosy café with a friendly retro atmosphere, comfortable old chairs, and decent coffee, teas and light meals. The savoury *palačinky* (crêpes) are a favourite. ⓐ Belgická 17 ⓣ 222 515 107 Ⓦ www.meduza.cz ⓛ 10.00–20.00 Ⓜ Metro: Náměstí Míru

Metropole £ ❻ Sleek, jazzy café with a chilled-out vibe offering sandwiches and other light snacks. ⓐ 18 Anny Letenské ⓣ 222 254 457 Ⓜ Metro: Náměstí Míru

Re Gourmet £ ❼ Good coffee while you shop for gourmet treats, such as marinated goat cheeses, sun-dried tomatoes and Italian breads. ⓐ Římská 29 ⓣ 222 515 391 ⓛ 10.00–19.00 Mon–Sat Ⓜ Metro: Náměstí Míru

U Dědka £ ❽ Chilled-out atmosphere for latte-sipping in the café upstairs or digging into some world foods downstairs. A menu to

---

❿ *Crawl up the Žižkov TV tower – or take the lift*

please all tastes, with cheap lunch specials. ⓐ Na Kozacce 12 ❶ 222 522 784 Ⓜ Metro: Náměstí Míru, then Tram: 4, 22 or 23 to Krymská

U Sadu £ ❾ A block from the TV Tower with everyday Czech dishes and antiques displayed at all angles. Its late opening hours make this a great stopover during a pub crawl. ⓐ Škroupovo náměstí 5 🕐 until 02.00 Ⓜ Metro: Jiřího z Poděbrad

Zanzibar £ ❿ Filling breakfasts and light savoury fare all day in a tastefully decorated space off a quiet square. Friendly service and a good wine list. ⓐ Americká 15 ❶ 222 520 315 🕐 08.00–23.00 Mon–Fri, 10.00–23.00 Sat & Sun Ⓜ Metro: Náměstí Míru

AFTER DARK

Restaurants
Palác Akropolis £ ⓫ One of Prague's best venues right under the Žižkov TV tower with a concert hall, restaurant, café and two bars under one roof. You'll come for the great food and drinks, and leave much later than you think! Ask the doorman to call you a taxi. ⓐ Kubelíkova 27 ❶ 296 330 913 Ⓦ www.palacakropolis.cz 🕐 café 10.00–24.00 Mon–Fri, 16.00–24.00 Sat & Sun; restaurant 11.30–01.00; bar 19.00–05.00 Ⓜ Metro: Jiřího z Poděbrad

Pivovarský Dům £ ⓬ A pub with its own microbrewery on site. Along with typical Czech-style beer, the company also brews fruit beers similar to those popular in Belgium. Good Czech restaurant serving all the classics, including Pivní sýr, a strong, pungent cheese that you mix with onions and a drop of beer to make a spread to eat on toasted bread. ⓐ Lipová 15 ❶ 296 216 666 🕐 11.00–23.30

Ⓦ www.gastroinfo.cz/pivodu Ⓝ Metro: IP Pavlova or Karlovo náměstí

Roma Pizza £ ⓭ This pizza joint outlasts even the latest of eaters. ⓐ Jagellonská 16 Ⓣ 222 714 154 Ⓛ 11.00–01.00 Ⓝ Metro: Jiřího z Poděbrad

Café Radost FX ££ ⓮ Prague's premier hot spot combines vegetarian dining in the restaurant, an underground house club, and a comfortable Asian-inspired lounge to take in the sights and sounds. A firm favourite with expats, locals and those in the know. Their wicked Sunday brunch is the best hangover cure on Earth. ⓐ Bělehradská 120 Ⓣ 224 254 776 Ⓦ www.radostfx.cz Ⓛ 10.00–03.00 Ⓝ Metro: IP Pavlova

Mosaika ££ ⓯ It may be outside the city centre, but it's worth the trip. International fusion with flair and an airy interior. ⓐ Nitranská 13 Ⓣ 224 253 011 Ⓛ 11.00–22.00 or later, if you want to finish that extra bottle Ⓝ Metro: Jiřího z Poděbrad, then Tram: 10 or 16 to Vinohradská vodárna

Clubs & bars
Gejzee..r The largest gay club in Prague is cavernous and sweaty with big dance floors and twin bars serving to all sorts, even straights. ⓐ Vinohradská 40 Ⓣ 222 516 036 Ⓛ 21.00–05.00 Thur–Sat Ⓝ Metro: Náměstí Míru

Hapu Friendly, unpretentious cocktails in cosy comfort. Get here early enough to get couch space. ⓐ Orlická 8 Ⓝ Metro: Flora, or Tram: 11 to Radhošťská

Le Clan As gloriously seedy as it gets, this spectacular DJ dive hits its stride in the wee hours with the drag queens and drug lords. If you can get past the dodgy characters at the door, head downstairs to meet other lounge lizards or move farther downstairs to play a quick game of ping pong. Mirrors in the toilets hang suspiciously horizontal. ⓐ Balbínova 23 ⓣ 222 251 226 ⓦ www.leclan.cz ⓜ Metro: Muzeum, or Tram: 11 to Italská

Stella This two-room space caters for both gays and lesbians with a dimly lit dance floor, a couple of couches, low prices and no flashy architectural elements. Stella has a neighbourhood vibe that attracts tourists and locals alike. ⓐ Lužická 10 ⓣ 224 257 869 ⓜ Metro: Nám. Míru

Termix One of the newer clubs to make the lesbian/gay scene, Termix is also one of the most popular. The lounge has a contemporary interior, modern glass bar, small dance floor, comfortable sofas and dark rooms. Admission and inhibition-free. Open late. ⓐ Třebízského 4 ⓣ 222 710 462 ⓛ 20.00–05.00 ⓜ Metro: Jiřího z Poděbrad

U vystřeleného oka The beers never cease at this thoroughly local pub that serves hearty and cheap grub to the mixed crowd of backpackers and yuppies. ⓐ U božích bojovníků 3 ⓣ 222 540 465 ⓛ 15.00–24.00 or later, depending on the thirst of the crowd ⓜ Metro: Florenc, then Tram: 5, 9 or 26 to Husinecká

▶ *Autumn colours in Karlštejn*

Karlštejn

Situated 29 km (18 miles) southwest of Prague, Karlštejn makes a perfect day trip from the city, as it's close enough to Prague for you to spend the day castle-gazing in the fresh air, and still make it back in time to enjoy the city nightlife. The magic of Karlštejn is that it's something typically Czech: a fairy-tale castle bang in the middle of some really gorgeous countryside. It's popular with tourists and Czechs alike, as evidenced by the visitor records – more than a quarter of a million people visit it each year – so try to arrive there early to beat the crowds.

Charles IV built the castle between 1348 and 1357 as a place of rest and relaxation, and as a fortress to safeguard the crown jewels of the Holy Roman Empire. In the period of Charles's reign, it took one day by horse to reach Prague, where the European political élite would meet. Through the hard work of renovation teams, what we see now is a perfectly preserved medieval castle, without any Gothic ornamentation.

The castle is a good place to visit, if you can get in on a tour, but just walking around its exterior is more than enough to capture the ambience of the place, especially if you're 'castled out' or simply aren't into chilly castle interiors. As you walk up the hill towards the castle you are immediately rewarded by the view spread out in front of you: picture-perfect rolling hills, the town and river. The townspeople have got used to seeing gaping visitors distractedly walking around, and many have set up shop right in their front yards, where you can browse and buy at your leisure.

GETTING THERE

By train

The best (and only) way to get to Karlštejn with public transport is by taking the train from Smíchov Station (Metro: Smíchovské nádraží). It leaves regularly throughout the day and takes about 45 minutes to reach Karlštejn.

By car

The quickest route by car takes about half an hour. Follow the E50 out of Prague, heading towards Plzen. Take the Beroun exit, and follow the signs along the Berounka River towards Karlštejn.

SIGHTS & ATTRACTIONS

Don't bother with the wax museum, Clock House, nativity museum or small fortress museum to be found in Karlštejn village. These are tourist traps and are not worth your while. Instead, go for a guided tour of **Karlštejn castle** which will take you through some interesting rooms and buildings. Tour One includes the Imperial Palace, Hall of Knights, Chapel of St Nicholas, Royal Bedroom and the Audience Hall. Tour Two includes all of Tour One plus the Holy Rood Chapel, the Chapel of St Katherine and Church of Our Lady, and the library.

The prismatic Great Tower with the **Holy Rood Chapel** is the most valuable part of the complex. Decorated by semi-precious stones, set in the shapes of crosses, the chapel holds a unique collection of idealised portraits of saints, popes, bishops and

◐ *Karlštejn – it's all uphill from here*

spiritual teachers. Above the altar there is a niche encased with golden bars, which once held the crown jewels and relics. Looking above, you see a starry sky with the moon and the sun and the five planets, the only ones known at that time.

You should book in advance by telephone or online if you wish to take Tour Two and visit the Holy Rood Chapel. Otherwise, you can buy tickets for the castle at the ticket information booth. Tour One costs 200 Kč for an adult, Tour Two is 300 Kč. Both have substantial discounts for students and children. The booth will also supply you with information about the town and events in the area.

🛈 274 008 154 🌐 www.hradkarlstejn.cz 🕐 09.00–12.00 & 12.30–17.00 Tues–Sun in May, June & Sept; 09.00–12.00 & 12.30–18.00 July & Aug; 09.00–12.00 & 13.00–16.00 Apr & Oct; 09.00–12.00 & 13.00–15.00 Nov, Dec & Mar

Karlštejn Golf Club

Established in 1993, Praha Karlštejn Golf Club hosted its first European PGA tour event in 1997. It serves up a challenging 18-hole, par-72 course on the hill just across the river from the castle with some truly magnificent views. It is one of the few courses in the Czech Republic that really challenges a golfer's ability. It's an uphill course, so be prepared to lug your clubs uphill between holes. It's a bit expensive by Czech standards (greens fees start at 1,400 Kč) but for golf enthusiasts, it's worth it. There's also an excellent relaxation centre with restaurant, swimming pool, hot steam room and massages so you can treat yourself after a hard day on the greens. Reservations are required for weekends.

🛈 311 604 991 🌐 www.karlstejn-golf.cz
🕐 08.00–sunset

TAKING A BREAK

Potraviny £ This grocery shop is the perfect place to stock up on picnic supplies for your wander in the woods along the Berounka River. It's on the right side of the main street as you go up the hill.
🕐 08.00–17.00 Mon–Sat

Hotel Restaurace Koruna £ Sit inside or out on the main street; the terrace tables are usually full of people feasting on the large portions of Czech fare and on the great views. Friendly staff.
🕐 311 681 465 🕐 09.30–22.00

🔺 *Bangles and baubles in Karlštejn's souvenir shops*

Restaurace U Janů £ A shady terrace and reasonable prices make this basic Czech restaurant a favourite. Live music at weekends.
☎ 311 681 210 🕐 09.30–22.00

Restaurace Blanky z Valois ££ On the main street heading up to the castle, this place serves pizzas and has an extensive wine list, though you should sample some of the quaffable Karlštejn vintage.
🕐 11.00–22.00

ACCOMMODATION

Hotel Elma £ Situated 3km from Karlštejn castle, this hotel offers reasonable prices and reasonable digs. Great views of the pretty Berounka river valley. ⓐ Srbsko 179 ☎ 311 622 974

Pension Pod dračí skálou £ Small and quaint with only three rooms, it's right under the dragon's cliff. ⓐ Karlštejn 130 ☎ 311 681 177

Hotel Koruna ££ This 3-star hotel is in the centre of Karlštejn and the management speaks English. The large summer terrace has lovely views of the castle. ⓐ Karlštejn 13 ☎ 311 681 341

Pension U Královny Dagmar ££ This 3-star budget option with friendly management is sure to please. ⓐ Karlštejn 2 ☎ 311 681 250

Romantický hotel Mlýn Karlštejn £££ A four-star treat in an old mill – the perfect place for a romantic overnight trip. The recently converted hotel is right on the riverbank and makes a good base for bike and canoe trips on the river. ⓐ Karlštejn 101 ☎ 311 744 411

▶ *The Holy Rood Chapel at Karlštejn*

Terezín (Theresienstadt)

Be warned: Terezín is a highly recommended and straightforward day trip from Prague, lying 48 km (30 miles) northwest of the city, but you will not want to linger for a nice lunch or stay overnight. In fact, after seeing what you'll see here, you'll want to ponder, and then leave. Even were it not for their barbaric use by the Nazis, the massive strongholds at Terezín (Theresienstadt in German) would still be a chilling sight.

Joseph II, son of Maria Theresa, built Terezín in 1866 as a fortress against Prussian attacks. The fortress was never used against the Prussians, so fell into disuse and was used alternately as a garrison and jail and a World War I POW camp. Then the occupying Nazi forces moved in.

Terezín, dubbed 'Paradise Ghetto' by the Nazis, was not a place of execution or medical testing; it was a transit camp through which more than 140,000 people passed: more than half ended up at the death camps of Auschwitz and Treblinka. A town originally built to garrison 5,000, Terezín held 60,000 inmates at the height of the war; 35,000 of these died from starvation, disease or suicide before they could be carted off in trains to the other concentration camps.

Terezín is a haunting reminder of the cruel public relations hoax that SS Chief Heinrich Himmler played on the rest of the world that was waking up to news of Nazi atrocities. In 1944, three foreign observers (two from the International Red Cross) came to Terezín to find out if the rumours of what was happening to the Jews were true. The Germans carefully choreographed every detail of the visit so that the observers saw a clean town with a Jewish administration, banks, shops, cafés, schools and a thriving cultural life. Plays, recitals, concerts and even a jazz band kept up the charade. To remedy the overcrowded conditions, the Nazis transported 7,500 of the camp's sick and elderly prisoners to Auschwitz. The observers left with the impression that all was well. The trick inspired the Nazis to make a film of the camp: *A Town Presented to the Jews from the Führer*. Russian forces liberated Terezín on 10 May 1945.

Today, the camp stands as a memorial to the dead and a monument to the dark side of humanity. But it is also an educational centre with a mission to educate people about this sad chapter in Czech history. Terezín Memorial staff became acutely aware of the absence of information regarding the

● *An aerial photo of the camp at Terezín*

Holocaust in Czech schools. In previous decades, under communism, the topic was taboo and experts were few. Now the educational centre offers well-researched study materials to young people and adults to re-open this chapter of history, focusing on themes of interpersonal relationships, tolerance and human dignity in the context of racial equality.

GETTING THERE

By car

Terezín is a 45-minute drive north out of Prague towards Dresden on the main highway E55 (D8). Look for the Terezín exit signs.

By bus

Six buses leave daily from Florenc bus station. The ride takes about an hour, a round-trip costs 40 Kč. Ⓦ www.vlak-bus.cz

Organised tours

Martin Tours provides a good, informative five-hour tour. Their bus leaves from Prague's Staroměstské náměstí and costs 1,100 Kč for an adult. ⓐ Stepánská 61 ⓣ 224 212 473 Ⓦ www.martintour.cz ⓛ tours leave at 09.30 Wed, Fri & Sun.

Wittmann Tours is an experienced company offering a seven-hour bus tour to the Terezín concentration camp. The bus leaves from Prague at Pařížská 28, near the Jewish Cemetery. The tour is 1,150 Kč per adult and free for children under 10. ⓐ Mánesova 8 ⓣ 222 252 472 Ⓦ www.wittmann-tours.com ⓛ tours leave at 10.00 daily May–Oct; 10.00 Tues, Thur, in Mar–Apr & Nov–Dec; private tours available Jan–Feb

ⓞ *A memorial to the victims of the Holocaust*

SIGHTS & ATTRACTIONS

The camp is what you come to Terezín to see. Inside the Major Fortress the plain, empty streets are eerie. Just off the main square lies the Museum of the Ghetto, chronicling the rise of Nazism and life in the camp. The exhibit provides English pamphlets to describe the exhibits. A ten-minute walk from the Major Fortress over the Ohře River takes you to the Minor Fortress. In front of the fortress's main entrance is the Národní hřbitov (National Cemetery), where the bodies exhumed from the mass graves were given proper burials. As you enter the main gate, the sign above it, 'Arbeit Macht Frei' ('Work Sets You Free'), is a depressing reminder of the self-righteousness that accompanied the appalling treatment of the people imprisoned here. You can walk through the Magdeburg prison barracks, execution grounds and cells. A combined entrance ticket gives you access to all parts of the camp and costs 180 Kč.
ⓐ Principova alej 304 ⓣ 416 782 225 ⓦ www.pamatnik-terezin.cz
ⓛ daily, except Christmas and New Year's Day; see website for opening hours of different areas of the camp

TAKING A BREAK

There are few places to eat in Terezín, and you may not want to stay here much longer than you have to. However, in the main parking lot you'll find a small stand where you can buy snacks and drinks. Inside the Major Fortress, near the museum, is a decent and inexpensive restaurant with standard Czech fare.
ⓛ 10.00–21.00 Sun–Fri

ⓓ *Rush-hour on Prague's metro*

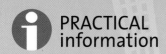

PRACTICAL
information

Directory

GETTING THERE
By air

Almost every international carrier or their affiliate serves Prague's Ruzyně Airport, not to mention low-cost air carriers like bmi baby, easyJet, and Smartwings and discount ticket agencies such as Fly Europe. The flight from England takes less than two hours. Check the following websites for incredible discounts, especially if you book more than a month in advance: www.bmibaby.com, www.easyjet.com, www.smartwings.com or www.flyeurope.com

Many people are aware that air travel emits CO_2 which contributes to climate change. You may be interested in the possibility of lessening the environmental impact of your flight through the charity Climate Care, which offsets your CO_2 by funding environmental projects around the world. Visit www.climatecare.org

By car

To get here from the UK by car, you will need to drive about 13 hours over 1,250 km (775 miles). For a detailed listing of your trip from start to finish, consult Ⓦ www.maporama.com

By bus

Coaches from the UK are equipped with toilets and reclining seats, and trips take about 20 hours. By law, drivers must stop at regular intervals for rest and refreshment. Here are two good companies, though there are quite a few:

Kingscourt Express operates the most popular and cheapest bus service at £68 round-trip. ⓐ Havelská 8 ⓘ 224 234 583 Ⓦ www.kce.cz

Eurolines/National Express offices offer regular coach services to Prague from London for about £88 round-trip. ⓐ 52 Grosvenor Gardens, London ⓦ www.nationalexpress.com

ENTRY FORMALITIES

As a member of the EU, the Czech Republic allows nationals of all EU countries, Australia, Canada, Japan, New Zealand, the USA and many other countries to visit the Czech Republic for up to 90 days without a visa. UK citizens can stay up to 180 days. South Africans are among those who must obtain a visa in their home country before arrival. To see what your current visa status is, visit www.mvcr.cz

MONEY & TAX REFUNDS

Money

The Czech Republic is a member of the EU, but the currency in Prague is still the Czech crown (CZK), or Kč, koruna českých. At current estimates, the euro will replace the crown by 2010. Banknotes come in denominations of 50, 100, 200, 500, 1,000, 2,000, 5,000 and 10,000 crowns. As in any other European capital, Prague has cash machines spread conveniently throughout the city. Use your Visa, MasterCard, Maestro, Visa Debit and American Express cards to withdraw cash from the ATMs of most Czech banks. If you have to exchange money, you can find the best rate at Xchange offices near the Old Town Square, or at any bank. There are many currency exchange offices dotting the tourist route of Prague, with varying exchange rates and commission charges, so ask what the final charge will be before you hand over your money. The following telephone numbers are useful if you lose a credit card:

American Express ℹ 224 194 400
MasterCard and Eurocard ℹ 224 423 135
Visa ℹ 224 125 353

Tax refunds

If you are a visitor from a non-EU country, you can reclaim up to
17 per cent of the value-added tax (DPH), provided you spend at
least 2,000 Kč in a single shop and stay in the Czech Republic for
fewer than 30 days. When paying the tax at the register, ask
for your receipt and a Tax-Free Shopping Envelope that you
will present to customs officials at the airport along with
the goods; you will receive a cheque in exchange. Once past
passport control, cash the cheque at the Tax-Free Refund Office.
There are refund offices at most major borders and in cities
across Europe as well. The refund programme does not apply
to art or antiques.

HEALTH, SAFETY & CRIME

The good news is: the water is safe to drink, and on 1 Jan 2006, the
Czech Republic introduced new anti-smoking laws which state that
smoking is prohibited at schools, cinemas, theatres, sports facilities,
state offices and other public spaces such as bus and tram stops.
Do not smoke while waiting for your tram; you will incur an on-the-
spot 1,000 Kč fine. When no-smoking sections will appear in bars
and restaurants is anyone's guess, and for the time being, you can
still light up there.

The bad news is: the air isn't safe to breathe on some days,
especially in the autumn and winter when smog settles over the
city. If you suffer from asthma, make sure you bring your inhaler
with you.

Prague is very safe to walk at all times of the day or night, and almost everyone uses public transport. Assaults are very rare, perhaps due to the visible police presence that tends to snuff out any problems before they arise. But Prague is a city, and therefore any tourist is a target. Pickpockets are very skilful, working in groups to distract and then immobilise unwary travellers as they ride the tram or underground metro. If a tram or underground metro compartment looks packed, don't squish in, just wait for the next train. If you go to a touristy restaurant or stay at a touristy hotel, watch for double-charging.

Swindles abound in Prague, but you'll be happy to know there's a way to fight back. If you've encountered waiters who voluntarily determine the tip by adding it to the bill, taxi drivers who overcharge or hotels that treat you badly, call the Česká Obchodní Inspekce (Czech Retail Inspection Office). The COI may not be able to help in your individual case but they can send out inspectors and can prevent it happening to others. Be sure to keep the receipt or note the details of the company involved when lodging a complaint. ⓐ Štěpánská 15 ⓣ 296 366 219 ⓦ www.coi.cz ⓛ 09.00–17.00 Mon–Fri

OPENING HOURS

Clothing shops and grocery stores in Prague are generally open Monday through Saturday from 10.00 to 18.00. Some close by 14.00 at weekends, and many others don't open on Sunday at all.

Restaurants are open generally every day from 11.00 to 22.00, but don't be surprised if they close earlier in winter.

Drinking pubs usually open every day at 17.00 and stay open at least until 23.00. Clubs stay open much longer, often until the wee hours of the morning.

TOILETS

There aren't many free public toilets in Prague and even McDonald's
charges to use the facilities. Unless you splash out for an admission

◆ *Petřín Hill in the springtime*

ticket to a cultural landmark or eat at a restaurant, you will have to cough up the whopping 5 Kč for your moment of porcelain, rough paper included. Pay toilets, labelled 'WC', are located at underground metro stations and along the tourist route.

CHILDREN

Prague is a very child-friendly city, with many parks to play in and child-oriented things to do and see. Prague's babies are well catered for, and you can find a wide variety of nappies and all sorts of baby accoutrements in any local baby shop or *drogerie* (drug store). Generally, the Czechs believe that children should be seen and not heard, and are not used to seeing them in fancy restaurants, expensive shops or at the opera. If you do decide to bring your small child to a cultural event, make sure that you are well armed with quiet anti-boredom ammunition to entertain them while you have fun. Another plus for children under six – entrance to most museums is free. If you are staying in Prague with your children and are not sure how to keep them entertained, here are a few activities that may do the trick.

- **Petřín Hill, Funicular, Mirror Maze & Observatory** The funicular ride to the top of Petřín Hill and the miniature Eiffel Tower is a big part of the fun, and once up, the *bludiště* (mirror maze) is a great diversion for both children and adults while the *Štefánikova hvězdárna* (observatory) can be of interest to older kids.

- **Prague Zoo** The Prague Zoo is located near the Trója Chateau on the outskirts of Prague and is open year round. The short chair-lift (with individual chairs) might be fun for older kids.

Admission is not too steep: 90 Kč for an adult, 60 Kč for children/students/seniors, and 270 Kč for a family. ⓐ U Trojského zámku 3/120 ⓦ www.zoopraha.cz ⓛ 09.00–17.00 Mar; 09.00–18.00 Apr, May, Sept & Oct; 09.00–19.00 Jun–Aug; 09.00–16.00 Nov–Feb ⓜ Metro: Nádraží Holešovice, then Bus: 112 to Zoologická zahrada (last stop)

● **Boat rides** You can take your kids on a boat ride on the Vltava, which seems to be the thing that all Prague families do on sunny summer weekends. A fun half-day activity is to take the 75-minute boat trip to the Zoo. Boats depart from Rašínovo nábřeží embankment (between the Palackého and Jiráskův bridges) at 09.30, 12.30 and 15.30 Mar–Oct. Tickets are 90 Kč for an adult,

△ *The kids will enjoy taking a pedalo on the Vltava*

60 Kč for a child over six, free for under-sixes. The boat also runs from the zoo back to the centre, departing at 11.00, 14.00 and 17.00.

- **Muzeum Hráček (Toy Museum)** The Toy Museum at the Prague Castle is the second largest exposition of toys in the world. ⓐ Jirska ul. 6 ⓦ www.barbiemuseum.cz 🕓 09.30–17.30 Apr–Nov Ⓝ Metro: Hradcanska

- **Nostalgická Tramvaj 91 (Nostalgic Tram No. 91)** This historic tram runs at weekends and holidays through all the most beautiful Prague locales from the end of March to mid-November. The tram leaves hourly from 12.00 to 18.00. With tickets costing 25 Kč for adults and 10 Kč for children and seniors, this is a cheap and cheerful way to cover a lot of ground without wearing out little legs. ⓐ Patočkova 4 ☎ 296 124 900

- *Divadla* **(Puppet shows)** Take the kids to see the famous **Divadlo Spejbla a Hurvínka (Spejbl and Hurvínek Theatre)**, full of silly stunts to keep you laughing. ⓐ Dejvická 38 ☎ 224 316 784 ⓦ www.spejbl-hurvinek.cz Ⓝ Metro: Hradčanská. The best of the black light theatre experiences can be found in the **Image Theatre**. ⓐ Pařížská 4 ☎ 222 314 448, 222 329 191 ⓦ www.imagetheatre.cz 🕓 box office 09.00–20.00 Mon–Sun Ⓝ Metro: Staroměstská

- **Parks** There are parks for children in the Malá Strana side of town. Kampa Park and Kampa Island right under Charles Bridge provide shady nap-time retreats, pedal boat rentals, and playgrounds.

COMMUNICATIONS

Public phones

Public telephones are either coin- or card-operated. You can buy
telephone cards in post offices, newsagents and kiosks or tobacco
stores. For international calls, you can buy a pre-paid card at the
above-mentioned places; this option costs significantly less than
using coins to make calls.

TELEPHONING THE CZECH REPUBLIC
Dialling code + 420 + local number (9-digit number)
Dialling codes:
Australia 0011
Canada 011
New Zealand 00
South Africa 09
UK 00
USA 011

TELEPHONING FROM THE CZECH REPUBLIC
00 + country code + local number
Dialling codes:
Australia 61
Canada 1
New Zealand 64
South Africa 27
UK 44
USA 1
International operator 1181

Mobile phones

Almost everyone has a mobile phone. The major mobile networks are Paegas, Eurotel and Oskar/Vodafone. If you decide to bring your mobile phone from home, make sure you enable your roaming programme so that you can receive calls once you're in Prague. Prague uses GSM 900/1800.

Internet

High-speed internet cafés dot the city, and these are the most central:

Blue Mail Internet café and gallery in the Old Town. ⓐ Konviktska 8 ⓛ 10.00–22.00 Mon–Fri, 10.00–23.00 Sat & Sun ⓝ Metro: Staroměstská

Bohemia Bagel Best bagels in town while you surf. You can also call abroad using its cheap, skype-like system. Two very central locations. ⓐ Masná 2 & Újezd 16 ⓣ 257 310 694 ⓦ www.bohemiabagel.cz ⓛ 07.00–24.00 ⓝ Metro: Staroměstská & Tram: 12, 22 or 23 to Újezd

Česká pošta (Czech Postal Service)

If you want to send packages back home, use the Main Post Office on Jindrišská 14 (ⓛ 06.00–22.00) across the street from the Obecní Dům (Municipal House). You can buy stamps at the post office, or any *tabák* (tobacconist) or information centre in town. Česká pošta post boxes are orange with two mail slots; you can put the mail in on either side. Costs for mailing are as follows:

Within Czech Republic letter or postcard 7.50 Kč

To Europe letter or postcard 9 Kč

To overseas airmail letter 14 Kč, airmail postcard 12 Kč

An airmail letter takes about a week to reach its overseas destination; a surface mail package could take up to three months to arrive.

ELECTRICITY

The electrical current is 220 V with standard, continental two-pin plugs and earthed, three-pin plugs. A two-pin plug will fit in a three-pin socket. Americans and Canadians with 110 V equipment will need a transformer that changes the voltage and an adapter to fit Czech sockets. Buy these adapters at any hardware or electronics store. British, Australians and South Africans can use a plug adapter which most department stores stock.

TRAVELLERS WITH DISABILITIES

Disabled visitors don't have it easy in Prague with its high kerbs and cobbled streets but things are changing. The Association of Disabled People (Sdružení zdravotně postižených 🅐 Praha 8, Karlínské nám. 12 🛈 224 816 997, ext. 238) can loan wheelchairs for 15–20 Kč per day or 700 Kč per month. They also have specially adapted cars that can be rented for 5 Kč per km.

Czech Railways (🛈 224 615 633) can pre-arrange transport at the stations and there are specially adapted carriages on selected trains. You should call four days in advance to make arrangements. More hotels, restaurants and cultural venues are introducing disabled access. Some metro stations have disabled access and these are all well-marked on most public transport/metro maps.

TOURIST INFORMATION

Czech Tourism The Official Czech Tourism Board. ⓐ Vinohradská 46
ⓣ 221 580 111 ⓕ 224 247 516 ⓦ www.czechtourism.cz ⓛ 09.00–16.30
Mon–Fri

PIS (Prague Information Service) Official telephone tourist
information. ⓣ 12 444 ⓦ www.pis.cz ⓔ tourinfo@pis.cz
ⓛ 08.00–19.00 Mon–Fri

You can find Prague Information Service offices at the following
locations:

ⓐ Main Railway Station ⓛ 09.00–19.00 Mon–Fri, 09.00–18.00 Sat &
Sun (summer); 09.00–18.00 Mon–Fri, 09.00–17.00 Sat & Sun
(winter)

ⓐ Malá Strana-Tower ⓛ 10.00–18.00 June, July & Aug

ⓐ Old Town Hall ⓛ 09.00–19.00 Mon–Fri, 09.00–18.00 Sat & Sun
(summer); 09.00–18.00 Mon–Fri, 09.00–17.00 Sat & Sun (winter)

BACKGROUND READING

Avant-Guide Prague–Insiders' Guide to Progressive Culture by
Dan Levine. A travel-book companion with attitude, and sharp,
insightful commentary on Prague's eateries, shops and clubs.
Prague in Black and Gold: The History of a City by Peter Demetz.
An interesting, in-depth look at the history of Prague from the
beginning.
Prague Tales by Jan Neruda. Melancholy stories that only Prague
could inspire.
The Spirit of Prague by Ivan Klíma. A well-constructed collection
relating the ironies and expectations of living in such a beautiful
place.
The Unbearable Lightness of Being by Milan Kundera. A psychological
foray into relationships at an uncertain time.

Useful phrases

Although English is widely spoken in the Czech Republic, these words and phrases may come in handy. See also the phrases for specific situations in other parts of the book.

English	Czech	Approx. pronunciation
BASICS		
Yes	Ano	Annoh
No	Ne	Neh
Please	Prosím	Prosseem
Thank you	Děkuji	Dekooyee
Hello	Dobry den	Dobree den
Goodbye	Nashledanou	Nazhlehdano
Excuse me	Promiňte	Prohminyteh
Sorry	Pardon	Pardohn
That's okay	Prima	Preemmah
To	Do	Doh
From	Od	Ohd
I don't speak Czech	Neumím česky	Neumeem cheskee
Do you speak English?	Umíte anglicky?	Oomeeteh anglitskee?
Good morning	Dobrý den	Dobree den
Good afternoon	Dobré odpoledne	Dobreh odpoledneh
Good evening	Dobrý večer	Dobree vecher
Good night	Dobrou noc	Dobrow nots
My name is ...	Jmenuji se ...	Menooyi sch ...

English	Czech	Approx. pronunciation
DAYS & TIMES		
Monday	Pondělí	Pondyelee
Tuesday	Úterý	Ootehree
Wednesday	Středa	Strzehda
Thursday	Čtvrtek	Chtvrtek
Friday	Pátek	Pahtek
Saturday	Sobota	Sobotah
Sunday	Neděle	Nedyele
Morning	Ráno	Rahno
Afternoon	Odpoledne	Odpoledneh
Evening	Večer	Vecher
Night	Noc	Nots
Yesterday	Včera	Vcherah

English	Czech	Approx. pronunciation
Today	Dnes	Dnehs
Tomorrow	Zítra	Zeetrah
What time is it?	Kolik je hodin?	Kollick yeh hodyin?
It is ...	Je ...	Yeh ...
09.00	Devět	Devyet
Midday	Poledne	Polledneh
Midnight	Půlnoc	Poolnots

NUMBERS

One	Jedna	Yednah
Two	Dvě	Dvyeh
Three	Tři	Trzhee
Four	Čtyři	Chteerzee
Five	Pět	Pyet
Six	Šest	Shest
Seven	Sedm	Sehdoom
Eight	Osm	Ohsoom
Nine	Devět	Devyet
Ten	Deset	Dessett
Eleven	Jedenáct	Yeddenahtst
Twelve	Dvanáct	Dvannahtst
Fifty	Padesát	Padehsaht
One hundred	Sto	Stoh

MONEY

I would like to change these traveller's cheques/this currency	Rád/Ráda bych vyměnil/ vyměnila tyto cestovní šeky/tuto měnu	Rahd/Rahdah bykh veemnyeneel/veemnyeneela teetoh tsestovnee shekyh/tutoh mnyenoo
Where is the nearest ATM?	Kde je nejbližší bankomat?	Gdeh yeh neyblishee bahnkomaht?
Do you accept traveller's cheques/credit cards?	Berete cestovní šeky/ kreditní karty?	Berretteh tsestovnee checkee/creditnee cartee?

SIGNS & NOTICES

Airport	Letiště	Letishtye
Railway station	Železniční stanice	Zheleznichnee stanyeetseh
Platform	Nástupiště	Nahstupishtye
Smoking/Non Smoking	Kuřáci/nekuřáci	Koorzahtsi/nekoorzahtsi
Toilets	Záchody	Zahkhodee
Ladies/Gentlemen	Dámy/Páni	Dahmee/Pahnee
Underground (Subway)	Metro	Metro

Emergencies

EMERGENCY TELEPHONE NUMBERS
Ambulance 155
Dental first aid 141 22
Emergency dispatching 112
Fire department 150
First aid 141 23
Municipal police 156
Pharmacy first aid 141 24
Police 158

MEDICAL SERVICES
Emergency treatment and non-hospital first aid are free for all visitors to the Czech Republic. You must pay for any other hospital care up front, but your insurance company will reimburse you when you return from your travels. British and EU nationals receive free health care (but not dental care) through a reciprocal agreement.

In an emergency, call 155, and an English-speaking operator should be provided. They will determine whether you need an ambulance or a taxi to take you to the nearest health facility. They will also explain your situation to the doctors, so there is no mistaking your condition. Remember to take your passport and some money with you in case you need to have a prescription made out immediately.

▶ *Pařížká Ulice at night*

Medical centres and clinics

These clinics offer a wide range of medical services in English. Most medical clinics will accept medical insurance and major credit cards, and many have an on-site pharmacy. It's a good idea to make an appointment before your visit; otherwise you could be waiting for hours.

Health Centre Prague 24-hour emergency service. Multilingual international staff, all branches of medicine. ⓐ Vodičkova 28 ⓣ 603 433 833 or 603 481 361 ⓦ www.doctor-prague.cz ⓛ 08.00–17.00 Mon–Fri ⓜ Metro: Můstek

Canadian Medical Care ⓐ Veleslavínská 1 ⓣ 235 360 133, 24-hour mobile GP 724 300 301 ⓦ www.cmc.praha.cz ⓛ 08.00–18.00 Mon–Fri ⓜ Metro: Dejvická, then Tram: 2, 20, 26 or 51 to Nádraží Veleslavín

American Dental Associates Top-notch care of your pearly whites. ⓐ Stará Celnice Building, 2nd Floor Atrium,V Celnici 4/1031 ⓣ 221 181 121 ⓛ appointments 08.00–18.00 Mon–Fri, 24-hour emergency care ⓜ Metro: Můstek

---

EMERGENCY PHRASES

Help! Pomoc! *Pommots!*   **Fire!** Hoří! *Horzee!*
Stop! Stop! *Stop!*

Call an ambulance/a doctor/the police/the fire brigade!
Zavolejte sanitku/doktora/policii/požárníky!
Zavoleyteh sanitkoo/doktorah/politsiyee/pozhahrneeckee!

POLICE STATIONS

Police stations have phone lines open 24 hours a day. The following are the most centrally located:

Police Headquarters @ Jungmannovo náměstí 9 ☎ 974 851 750

@ Bartolomějská 14, Old Town ☎ 974 851 700

@ Vlašská 3, Lesser Quarter ☎ 974 851 730

@ Benediktská 1, New Town ☎ 974 851 710

LOST PROPERTY

Lost and Found Office @ Karoliny Světlé 5 ☎ 224 235 085 Ⓜ Metro: Národní Třída

EMBASSIES AND CONSULATES

Australian Consulate @ Klimentská ul.10, 6th Floor ☎ 296 578 350 🕐 08.30–17.00 Mon–Thur, 08.30–14.00 Fri Ⓜ Metro: Florenc

Canadian Embassy @ Muchova 6 ☎ 272 101 800 @ canada@canada.cz 🕐 08.30–12.30 & 13:30–16.30 Mon–Fri Ⓜ Metro: Hradčanská

New Zealand Consulate @ Dykova 19 ☎ 222 514 672 ⓦ www.nzconsul.cz 🕐 09.00–13.00 & 14.00–17.30 Mon–Thur Ⓜ Metro: Jiřího z Poděbrad

South African Consulate @ Ruská 65 ☎ 267 311 114 or 271 731 799 🕐 08.30–12.00 Mon–Fri Ⓜ Metro: Želívského

UK Embassy @ Thunovska 14 ☎ 257 402 111 @ consular/visa.prague@fco.gov.uk 🕐 08.30–17.00 Mon–Thur, 08.30–16.00 Fri Ⓜ Metro: Malostranská

United States Embassy @ Tržiště 15 ☎ 257 530 640 @ aic@usembassy.cz 🕐 13.00–16.00 Mon–Thur Ⓜ Metro: Malostranská

The publishers would like to thank the following individuals and organisations for supplying their copyright photos for this book.
Carolyn Zukowski: pages 1, 5, 7, 18–19, 25, 29, 30, 37, 38, 65, 71, 91, 108, 121, 131
Czech Tourism: pages 10, 12–13, 14, 16, 21, 22, 40–41, 43, 44, 47, 50, 55, 59, 63, 74, 79, 87, 97, 100, 104, 111, 116, 125, 128, 133, 135, 136, 139, 144, 146, 155
Helena Zukowski: pages 83, 85

Copy editor: Anne McGregor
Proofreader: Lynn Bresler

Send your thoughts to
books@thomascook.com

- **Found a great bar, club, shop or must-see sight that we don't feature?**

- **Like to tip us off about any information that needs updating?**

- **Want to tell us what you love about this handy little guidebook and more importantly how we can make it even handier?**

Then here's your chance to tell all! Send us ideas, discoveries and recommendations today and then look out for your valuable input in the next edition of this title. As an extra 'thank you' from Thomas Cook Publishing, you'll be automatically entered into our exciting monthly prize draw.

Send an email to the above address (stating the book's title) or write to: CitySpots Project Editor, Thomas Cook Publishing, PO Box 227, The Thomas Cook Business Park, Unit 18, Coningsby Road, Peterborough PE3 8SB, UK.